Latin American–U.S. Economic Relations, 1982–1983

T0383957

Also of Interest

†*Latin American Nations in World Politics,* edited by Heraldo Muñoz and Joseph S. Tulchin

†*The Third World Coalition in International Politics,* Second Updated Edition, Robert A. Mortimer

The Exclusive Economic Zone: A Latin American Perspective, edited by Francisco Orrego Vicuña

Mexico's Dilemma: The Political Origins of Economic Crisis, Roberto Newell G. and Luis Rubio F.

Change in Central America: Internal and External Relations, edited by Wolf Grabendorff, Heinrich-W. Krumwiede, and Jörg Todt

†*Latin America and the U.S. National Interest: A Basis for U.S. Foreign Policy,* Margaret Daly Hayes

Sovereignty in Dispute: The Falklands/Malvinas, 1943–1982, Fritz L. Hoffmann and Olga Mingo Hoffmann

†*Latin America, Its Problems and Its Promise: A Multidisciplinary Intro-duction,* edited by Jan Knippers Black

†*FOREIGN POLICY on Latin America, 1970–1980,* edited by the staff of *Foreign Policy*

†*The Caribbean Challenge: U.S. Policy in a Volatile Region,* edited by H. Michael Erisman

U.S.-Panama Relations, 1903–1978: A Study in Linkage Politics, David Farnsworth and James McKenney

†Available in hardcover and paperback.

Latin American–U.S. Economic Relations, 1982–1983

Sistema Económico Latinoamericano/
Latin American Economic System

Routledge
Taylor & Francis Group

LONDON AND NEW YORK

First published 1984 by Westview Press, Inc.

Published 2018 by Routledge
52 Vanderbilt Avenue, New York, NY 10017
2 Park Square, Milton Park, Abingdon, Oxon OX14 4RN

Routledge is an imprint of the Taylor & Francis Group, an informa business

Library of Congress Cataloging in Publication Data
Relaciones económicas de América Latina con
Estados Unidos, 1982–1983. English.
Latin American–U.S. economic relations, 1982–1983.
Translation of: Relaciones económicas de América
Latina con Estados Unidos, 1982–1983.
Includes index.
1. United States—Foreign economic relations—Latin
America. 2. Latin America—Foreign economic relations—
United States. 3. United States—Foreign economic
relations. 4. United States—Economic policy—
1981– . I. Sistema Económico Latinoamericano.
HF1456.5.L3R4413 1984 337.7308 84-7464
ISBN 13: 978-0-367-00530-6 (hbk)
ISBN 13: 978-0-367-15517-9 (pbk)

Contents

Tables and Charts

Charts

Introduction

Latin America's economic relations with the United States have been analyzed on numerous occasions within the framework of SELA (Sistema Económico Latinoamericano), as reflected in a number of decisions adopted by the Latin American Council, especially the Panama declaration, endorsed in Decision 114, which resulted from the 1981 high-level consultations on Latin America's economic relations with the United States.

The Panama declaration contains a number of criteria and objectives that Latin American countries should establish and promote in the context of their relations with the United States. Furthermore, it identifies a number of measures relating to trade, commodities, financing, transnational enterprises, foreign investment, and the transfer of technology, and outlines the need to compile, analyze, and evaluate data on the various aspects of these relations, with a view to facilitating coordinated action among Latin American nations.

This volume analyzes U.S. international economic policy and the interactions involved in its formulation. It discusses, among other issues, the effects of U.S. policy on Latin American economies and trade relations and the policies of international financial agencies. Chapter 1 deals with U.S. domestic economic policy; Chapter 2 explores the international repercussions of this policy; and Chapter 3 analyzes current economic relations between Latin America and the United States and presents conclusions and recommendations on possible concerted action by Latin American nations. Finally, the Annex evaluates the U.S. decision-making process.

1

U.S. Economic Policy:
The Internal Dimension

The State of the U.S. Economy
Toward the End of the Seventies

The problems facing the U.S. economy are not new. On 15 August 1971, President Richard Nixon announced his new economic policy as the "broadest attempt . . . made in four decades" to "achieve a higher level of employment, greater price stability and a more solid international position for the nation."[1] Almost a decade later, President Ronald Reagan outlined his Economic Recovery Program (ERP) to Congress as follows:

> I have painted a discouraging picture, but I believe that I am correct. It is within our power to change this picture and we can act accordingly. . . . We have an economic recovery program, one which will balance the budget and place us decisively on the path to achieving our ultimate goals of completely eliminating inflation, increasing productivity and creating millions of new jobs.[2]

The seventies was a period of clear deterioration in the performance of the U.S. economy, at least in comparison with the two and a half decades following the Second World War. This decline involved slow and unstable economic growth accompanied by high levels of unemployment, increasing difficulty in controlling inflationary pressures, and a significant decline in the productivity growth rate. From 1974 to 1980, the real gross national product (GNP) grew at a rate of 2.5 percent per annum, whereas from the end of the forties to the beginning of the seventies the average rate had been 4 percent. As measured by the growth of the consumer price index, inflation rose from 3 percent in 1974 to 8 percent in 1980.

The productivity growth rate decreased from 2.5 percent in 1970 to −0.1 percent per annum in 1979–1981 (see Table 1). If, as has been suggested by some observers, a "poverty index" were created by adding inflation and unemployment rates, a significant decline would be recorded for the last part of the seventies (see Chart 1).

Added to this overall performance were the effects of decreased competition in the postwar U.S. economy within such key sectors as the steel industry, the auto industry, and other producers of durable and nondurable consumer goods. These developments caused economic and political tensions that were further aggravated by a general stagnation in productivity.

The external sector also began to show signs of significant transformation and growing instability, which resulted in trade deficits in all but three years: 1970, 1973, and 1975. At the same time, as shown in Table 2, the surplus derived from profit remittances · and other services showed significant gains that partially compensated for the adverse effects of merchandise trade on the current account balance. Capital movements also fluctuated significantly during the seventies. The widespread adoption of variable exchange rates in 1973 did not substantially check this trend toward growing instability in the external sector.

As the U.S. economy opened up, international economic phenomena began to play a more significant role in the evaluation of the domestic economy. Exports, which had averaged 3.9 percent of the gross national product between 1965 and 1969, doubled to 7.6 percent between 1978 and 1982. This openness significantly modified the United States' traditional economic links with the rest of the world. It also made the dollar vulnerable to short-term international capital movements (associated with the development of an international market deprived of capital), which on several occasions called for economic policy measures to uphold the international standing of the U.S. dollar. The steps taken by the Carter administration in November 1978 provide one example.

Table 1. Postwar U.S. Economic Performance, 1947–1982

	1947–57	1957–67	1967–73	1973–82[a]
Demand (Annual growth rates, %)				
Nominal GNP	6.7	6.0	8.6	9.7
Money (M_2)	2.8	5.8	8.6	9.7
Rate of M_2	3.9	0.2	0.0	0.0
Real GNP	3.8	4.0	3.4	1.8
Nondurable consumption	2.9	3.7	2.1	1.9
Durable consumption and household investment	4.3	3.9	7.6	−0.3
Nonhousehold fixed investment	3.0	4.6	4.0	2.0
Federal outlays	9.5	3.4	−4.3	2.1
State and local expenditure	6.0	5.8	3.6	1.1
Real government transfers to individuals	3.5	7.4	10.0	5.4
Supply (Annual growth rates, %)				
Real private sector GNP	3.5	4.5	3.7	1.8
Hours	0.3	1.3	1.6	1.0[b]
Output per hour	3.2	3.2	2.1	0.1[b]
GNP deflator	2.9	2.0	5.2	7.7
Average Values (%)				
Unemployment rate				
Mean	4.3	5.3	4.7	7.0
Standard deviation	1.0	1.0	1.0	1.4
Nonhousehold fixed investment/GNP	9.7	9.7	10.2	10.8
Government outlays/GNP	22.6	26.4	29.7	30.8
Goods and services	18.5	20.8	21.8	19.8
Transfer payments	4.1	5.6	7.9	11.0

[a]Figures for 1982 are provisional.
[b]Nonagricultural private sector.

Sources: Robert J. Gordon, "Postwar Macroeconomics: The Evolution of Events and Ideas," in M. Feldstein, *The American Economy in Transition* (Chicago: University of Chicago Press, 1980); Office of the President, *Economic Report of the President,* 1983 (Washington, D.C.: GPO, 1983).

Chart 1. "Poverty Index" of Unemployment and Inflation Rates (%)[a]

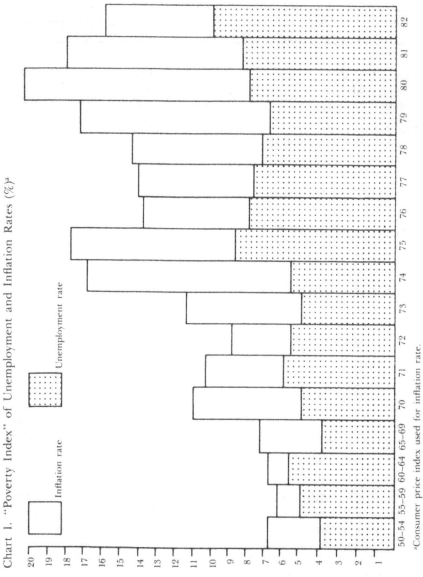

[a]Consumer price index used for inflation rate.

Source: U.S., Office of the President, Economic Report of the President, 1983 (Washington, D.C.: GPO, 1983).

Table 2. U.S. International Transactions, 1960–1982 (net balances in billions US$)

	1960–64	1965–69	1970	1971	1972	1973	1974	1975	1976	1977	1978	1979	1980	1981	1982[a]
Merchandise	5.4	2.8	2.6	−2.3	−6.4	0.9	−5.3	9.0	−9.3	−30.9	−33.7	−27.3	−25.3	−27.9	−32.0
Investment income	4.2	5.5	6.2	7.2	8.2	12.2	15.5	12.8	16.0	18.0	20.6	31.2	29.9	33.0	29.0
Military transactions	2.4	2.9	−3.3	−2.9	−3.4	−2.1	−1.6	−0.7	0.6	1.5	0.6	−2.0	−2.5	−1.5	1.0
Travel and transport	−1.1	−1.5	−2.0	−2.3	−3.1	−3.2	−3.2	−2.8	−2.6	−3.3	−3.1	−2.4	−0.9	−0.2	0.0
Other services	0.8	1.6	2.2	2.5	2.8	3.2	4.0	4.6	4.7	5.2	6.0	5.7	7.1	7.7	8.0
Balance of goods and services	6.8	5.4	5.6	2.3	−1.9	11.0	9.3	22.9	9.4	−9.4	−9.7	5.1	8.3	11.1	6.0
Unilateral transfers	−2.6	−3.0	−3.3	−3.7	−3.8	−3.9	−7.2	−4.6	−5.0	−4.6	−5.0	−5.6	−6.8	−6.6	7.0
Current account bal.	4.2	2.4	2.3	1.4	−5.8	7.1	2.1	18.3	4.4	−14.1	−14.8	−0.5	1.5	4.5	−1.0
U.S. assets abroad (− outflow)	−6.1	−9.1	−9.3	−12.5	−14.5	−22.9	−34.7	−39.7	−51.3	−34.8	−61.1	−64.3	−86.0	−109.3	−127.0
Foreign assets in the U.S. (+ inflows)	2.7	6.9	6.4	23.0	21.5	18.4	34.2	15.7	36.5	51.3	64.0	38.5	54.5	77.9	94.0
SDR[b] allotments	—	—	0.9	0.7	0.7	—	—	—	—	—	—	1.1	1.1	1.1	—
Statistical dif.	−0.9	−0.2	−0.2	−9.8	−1.9	−2.6	−1.6	5.7	10.4	2.5	11.9	25.2	28.9	25.8	34.0

[a]First three quarters of 1982.
[b]SDR = special drawing rights.

Source: Office of the President, Economic Report of the President, 1983 (Washington, D.C.: GPO, 1983).

The last decade witnessed what was then considered to be the worst and most prolonged recession since the thirties. This was followed by a five-year period of economic recovery characterized by unstable and ineffectual performance patterns. The recovery ended with a brief but severe recession in 1980. That year, real GNP fell at an annual rate of 0.4 percent, and the economy was extremely unstable in the middle of 1980.[3] The unemployment rate increased from an average of 5.8 percent in 1979 to a high of 7.8 percent in July 1980, falling again to 7.3 percent in December of the same year. According to the consumer price index, inflation increased from 11.3 percent in 1979 to 13.5 percent the following year.[4]

The 1980 recession brought substantial fluctuations and a general increase in interest rates. Short-term rates for three-month treasury bills increased from an average of 10 percent in 1979 to 11.5 percent in 1980. During 1980, variations ranged from 15.5 percent in the month of March to 6.9 percent in June, increasing again to 15.7 percent in December.

The final months of the Carter administration were characterized by a weak real economy, fluctuating but generally high interest rates, an increase in the cost of the dollar, relatively stable inflation, and increased unemployment. Indeed, the 1980 recession was closely related to a series of events that occurred during the previous year, three of which will be mentioned here.

1. A second shock in the oil industry resulted from the reduced supply from Iran due to that country's domestic problems. Efforts to increase inventories and maintain a stable supply pushed up the purchase price for U.S. refineries by 94 percent in 1979. The Council of Economic Advisors estimated that the loss in potential production from the increase in oil prices represented about 2 percent of U.S. GNP.

2. Economic policy was concentrated on controlling the inflationary impact that would eventually follow the increase in oil prices. The "high employment budget deficit," which declined in 1978 by $8.1 billion, was further reduced by $12.8 billion in 1979.[5] Added to these deflationary measures were a decrease in monetary supply and a sustained increase in short-term interest rates. These monetary restrictions were closely related to the modifications introduced in October 1979 by the Federal Reserve Board in its monetary policy.

In accordance with its new procedure, the board was able to control increases in bank reserves to make them compatible with growth objectives with regard to monetary stock, but it abandoned all efforts to control interest rates. Thus, the Federal Reserve not only brought about important increases in interest rates in the short run, but also had to accept much greater fluctuations in these interest rates.

3. Financial imbalances at the individual level made a contraction in consumer expenditure likely. As a result of advance purchases in anticipation of inflation, consumers increased expenditure at a rate higher than the increase in disposable income, causing savings levels to contract.[6] Signs of deterioration in the financial situation of individual consumers included a sustained increase in debts and an increasingly high rate of unrepaid loans to finance consumption.

In short, 1980 was a poor year for economic performance. The most violent contraction in economic activity since the postwar period was recorded in the second quarter, followed by a modest recovery during the second half of the year. In this latter period, the maintenance of restrictive monetary conditions again pushed up interest rates, which had fallen due to the contraction in demand for credit, in turn a result of the recession and selective controls introduced by the Federal Reserve between the months of March and July of 1980. Throughout 1980 the rate of price increases dropped slightly.

The Theoretical Basis of
the Reagan Administration's Economic Policy

In November 1980, the Republican party gained a majority in the Senate, reduced its minority in the House of Representatives, and placed its presidential candidate, Ronald Reagan, in the Oval Office. From the outset, the new administration stressed the priority that it would assign to economic affairs during its mandate. Indeed, discussions concerning the state of the economy and economic policy alternatives became the central theme of the 1980 electoral debate, forming a solid base on which Ronald Reagan built his decisive victory.

Ronald Reagan entered the White House with a clear mandate to pursue a conservative philosophy and economic policy, presented as a clear break from traditional postwar economic policy. The new administration viewed stagflation—the "presence of progressively increasing inflation and unemployment rates"[7]—as the main problem facing the country. Responsibility for this state of affairs was laid on the economic policy pursued during the greater part of the postwar period, and the consequent increase in federal government activity and intervention in the economy. The emphasis of the new economic policy would be to reverse these trends by reducing government intervention in the various areas of the economic process (fiscal policy, monetary policy, and regulatory policy). This was the basis for Reagan's Economic Recovery Program.

The ERP follows several fundamental analytical principles. In general terms, the program falls into the category of traditional, classic economic policy. It emphasizes reduction in government intervention as a means of improving economic performance, while underlining the need to balance public finances and develop restrictive monetary policies. Added to these conventional measures were others taken from relatively recent developments in economic theory. One theory assumed that the costs of moving from a system with high inflation to one with a slower rate could be substantially offset if the expectations of the economic agents were adjusted with sufficient speed. For this to occur, the economic authorities had to supply private agents with adequate information and a consistent policy line. The second measure—in fact a reformulation of Say's law—could be classified as the "new orthodoxy" advanced by the supply siders. According to these economists, a reduction in marginal tax rates would serve as a great incentive to economic activity. These effects would not be felt on the demand side—as traditional Keynesian policy would assert—but rather, through a reestablishment of incentives and supply motivation.

The first assumption behind the ERP was the rejection of the notion prevailing in the sixties—during the boom of the "New Economics"—that economic activity could be protected from extreme fluctuations through proper management of aggregate demand (fine-tuning). Control of the instruments of economic policy would introduce compensatory movements into government expenditure, to offset fluctuations in other expenditure components such as private investment and external demand. The Phillips curve suggested that society or policymakers could choose the optimum combination of inflation and unemployment through fine-tuning. As inflation and unemployment moved in inverse relation to each other, fine-tuning became the ideal instrument for maintaining conditions of long-term full employment. The only drawback was the cost associated with the inflation rate.

The implicit assumption in postwar economic policy of an inverse relationship between inflation and unemployment was also rejected by the new administration. According to changes introduced into the Phillips curve paradigm, principally by monetarists,[8] this inverse relationship would disappear in the long run. Therefore, fine-tuning could only affect the unemployment level in the short run, depending on the rate of adjustment of inflationary expectations and the cost of constantly rising inflation. In the long run, as expectations reached equilibrium, unemployment would return to its "natural" level and the only effect of this economic policy on society would be a higher inflation rate.

In short, fine-tuning would only affect monetary variables (inflation rate), leaving real variables such as the unemployment rate untouched. These would then settle at their long-term equilibrium level (the "natural unemployment rate"). Consequently, the coexistence of the increasing inflation and unemployment rates (stagflation) of the seventies was thought to be the result of efforts at excessive fine-tuning. At the same time, the equilibrium mechanisms of the labor market were being hindered by a series of government regulations that only served to increase the natural unemployment rate—measures such as minimum wage legislation and unemployment insurance. The only way to reduce the equilibrium level of unemployment was to remove the institutional barriers that made adjustment to labor market equilibrium positions difficult. Inflation would also be contained by abandoning any systematic attempt at controlling the real variables of the economy.

This reasoning formed part of the economic cycle theory of which stop-and-go policies were an essential component.

Repeated attempts to utilize monetary and fiscal policy to stimulate production—whilst affirming that inflation would be contained in the future—only resulted in even higher inflation rates. These attempts also created expectations regarding future trends. The inflexibility of expectations of higher inflation rates in the future resulted in policymakers introducing further economic restrictions, thus creating a new recession, followed in turn by renewed efforts to stimulate economic activity. In short, both policy and stop-and-go economic performance cycles were being repeated.[9]

There is much skepticism as to the effectiveness of economic policy measures associated with monetarism. From an extreme point of view, a "straight" fiscal policy—that is, the independent financing of fiscal activities by a monetary policy—only means moving expenditure from the private to the public sector of the economy (crowding out). This is done either directly (tax collection) or indirectly (effect on interest rates). The economy is affected if bonds are issued to finance part of the fiscal exercise, although in the long run only the monetary variables will feel this effect. For this reason, the relevant component of economic policy is monetary policy, which is nevertheless unable to affect the real sector in the long run.

The stability trend inherent in the real economy via the price mechanism is a central component of this paradigm. External shocks are only intensified by the compensatory economic policy, which in turn diminishes the effectiveness of the markets' self-regulatory mechanisms. For this reason, the economic policy should not include anticyclical factors but should be based on constant norms applicable to the growth rate of the money stock. Fiscal policy should help to reduce the pressure on the monetary policy caused by the financing of demands. The level of state activity, given its inherent inefficiency, should be controlled. One priority of the ERP is therefore the development of a stable and credible medium-term economic policy. The greater the confidence and information among economic agents with respect to the government policy, the speedier the adjustment of expectations (and transition) from a high-inflation to a low-inflation economy.

The ERP also contains the analytical assumptions of the supply siders. This school of economists disagrees with monetarists, who, like the Keynesians, give priority to analysis of demand. Supply siders, on the other hand, emphasize the conditions of supply as the determining factor of economic evolution. Supply siders do share some of the monetarists' concerns and assumptions about the highly monetary nature of inflation and the notion of stability in the real sector of the economy. However, their priorities in economic policy differ. Tax policy is the focal point for supply siders, who believe it affects relative prices (and consequently the relation between work and leisure, consumption and savings) more than the aggregate demand. The tax policy is thus an essential determinant of production because it marginally affects individual decisions and decisively influences the supply of productive factors.

According to the supply siders, a reduction in marginal tax rates will restore production and savings incentives, thus reconstituting the basic mechanisms of the economic thrust. An extreme point of view (made popular by the Laffer curve) is that the positive effect on incentives will produce an increase in real production sufficient to multiply fiscal income. In this way, tax reductions would be self-financing and would even reduce the fiscal deficit. Even if the deficit were not totally eliminated, the relative prices favorable to savings would provide the necessary financing.

The supply siders share the monetarists' view that an anticyclical policy in managing the aggregate demand is extremely destabilizing. They also suggest the superiority of fixed rules of economic policy. Within this new orthodoxy, inflation is seen as a strictly monetary phenomenon, and supply siders therefore recommend a restrictive policy. To free monetary policy from political pressures, they propose the reestablishment of the gold standard as a means of controlling monetary flows. The classic dichotomy between real and monetary phenomena is taken to an extreme in this case, as shown by the asserted possibility of promoting rapid economic growth through fiscal policy (tax reduction) within the framework of decreasing inflation (restrictive monetary policy).

The economic policy recommendations of supply siders undoubtedly hinged on political rather than economic reasoning. Implicit in their attitude toward fiscal policy was the understanding that arguments favorable to a reduction in public expenditure are not politically viable. A proposal for tax reductions was more likely to be politically acceptable, particularly in the context of the tax upheaval experienced in the United States at the end of the seventies.

Finally, both the supply siders and the monetarists were critical of increased state activity. Two premises were therefore central to the ERP: (1) "the economies of all nations having a widely representative government and civil rights to a large extent are market oriented"; and (2) "the economic situation of market economies is normally superior to that of other nations [with comparable culture and resources] in which the government plays the dominant role."[10]

Both statements are based on the assumption that the market, through the price mechanism, is the ideal instrument for efficient allocation of a society's resources. Political involvement in this allocation creates imbalances due to interest group pressure, and it distorts relative prices because of the need to finance government intervention. Moreover, market operations stimulate cooperation in the quest for overall positive results; taxation causes conflict, evasion, or the development of a clandestine economy.

Government intervention to prevent occasional defects in the market operation (exogenous factors, monopolies, state procurement, fairness and redistribution factors) may be even more costly than the distortions to be corrected. Thus, government intervention would best stimulate market functioning by adjusting and interfering with relative prices as little as possible.

In short, the ERP was inspired by two schools of economic orthodoxy that were in themselves contradictory. The emphasis on limiting state activity, restricting monetary policy, and creating incentives was linked to a medium-term perspective. The program's stability and its credibility among economic agents would determine the speed with which expectations would be adjusted. The sooner this occurred, the less the transition costs. The ERP was therefore seen as substantially modifying the content and operational assumptions of the economic policy prevailing during the greater part of the postwar period.

Fiscal Policy

The two basic elements of fiscal policy included in the ERP are a budgetary reform plan to reduce the growth rate of federal expenditure; and a series of proposals for a 10 percent annual reduction in income tax over a period of three years and for the creation of additional jobs through a system of accelerated depreciation in company investment in plants and equipment.[11]

We shall first present the proposal for public expenditure in its original form. The predominant view of the administration was that the rapid increase in public expenditure was one of the main factors behind the recession and inflation prevailing in the United

Table 3. Growth in U.S. Federal Expenditure, 1955–1984

	1955–64	1976–81	1979–81	1982–84
Annual growth rate (%)				
Total expenditure	6.3	11.9	15.9	5.6
National defense	2.9	11.9	17.0	16.5
Nondefense	9.9	12.0	15.5	1.7
Average % of GNP				1984
Total Expenditure	18.7	22.1	22.3	18.8[a]
National defense	9.4	5.3	5.3	6.1[a]
Nondefense	9.3	16.8	17.0	12.7[a]

[a]Personal estimate. The calendar years do not coincide with the fiscal years.

Source: America's New Beginning: A Program for Economic Recovery, Presidential message to Congress on the occasion of the presentation of the ERP, 18 February 1981 (Washington, D.C.: GPO, 1981); Office of the President, *Economic Report of the President,* 1983 (Washington, D.C.: 1983).

States. To alleviate the effects of this rise in expenditure, the ERP proposed the following measures:

- a reduction in the 16 percent annual growth rate in federal expenditure to an average of 7 percent up to 1986 (see Table 3)
- a significant reallocation of funds, giving priority to defense, with the annual growth rate increasing to 8 percent for the next five years (see Table 4)
- a reduction in the entitlement programs such as food stamps, increased workers' benefits, loans, various secondary social security benefits, and Medicaid (see Table 4)
- reduction of a broad range of federal programs considered to be inefficient or unessential, such as energy research development, the Employment and Training Act, the development of synthetic fuel, and the Export-Import Bank
- a systematic reduction in the public deficit resulting in a balanced budget in 1984 and modest surpluses thereafter (see Table 5).

Table 4. Budget Priorities of the Economic Recovery Program

	1962	1981	1984
Expenditure in billions US$			
Defense Department,			
military expenditure	46.8	157.9	249.8
Social safety net programs	26.2	239.3	313.0
Net interest on the			
public debt	6.9	64.3	66.8
Other programs	26.9	193.2	142.0
Total	106.8	654.7	771.6
Percentage of total expenditure			
Defense Department,			
military expenditure	43.8	24.1	32.4
Social safety net programs	24.5	36.6	40.6
Net interests	6.4	9.8	8.6
Other programs	25.2	29.5	18.4
Total	100.0a	100.0	100.0

aFigures do not add up due to rounding.

Source: America's New Beginning: A Program for Economic Recovery, Presidential message to Congress on the occasion of the presentation of the ERP, 18 February 1981 (Washington, D.C.: GPO, 1981).

Table 5. U.S. Federal Expenditure and Income, 1981–1986 (billions US$)

Fiscal year	Income	Expenditure	Deficit (−) Surplus (+)
1981	600.2	654.7	−54.5
1982	650.5	696.5	−46.0
1983	710.1	733.1	−23.0
1984	772.1	771.6	0.5
1985	851.0	844.0	7.0
1986	942.1	912.1	30.0

Source: America's New Beginning: A Program for Economic Recovery, Presidential message to Congress on the occasion of the presentation of the ERP, 18 February 1981 (Washington, D.C.: GPO, 1981).

Table 6. Public Expenditure as a Percentage of GNP

Fiscal year	Percentage
1981	23.0
1982	21.8
1983	20.4
1984	19.3
1985	19.2
1986	19.0

Source: America's New Beginning: A Program for Economic Recovery, Presidential message to Congress on the occasion of the presentation of the ERP, 18 February 1981 (Washington, D.C.: GPO, 1981).

In short the ERP proposed a substantial modification of the trends prevailing during the last decade and a half, reducing the growth of public expenditure while making a large-scale reallocation of resources to defense. The ERP projected a sustained decrease in the share of public spending in GNP as a result of these recommendations and the expected performance of the real economy (see Table 6).

According to the original program, the benefits aimed at supporting the low-income sectors within the social security system would not be affected. The social safety net programs include Medicare; basic unemployment benefits; complementary security benefits for the elderly and handicapped; veterans' benefits and services; and insurance for the disabled, the elderly, widows, widowers, and others. About 93 percent of these benefits are covered by programs linked to the social security system and financed by income tax deductions.

These recommendations on public expenditure were linked to a bold tax reduction policy that included a 10 percent annual reduction in personal income tax rates over a three-year period as of 1 July 1981 and accelerated depreciation of fixed assets for tax purposes as of 1 January 1981.

The first measure would move the marginal income tax rates from a range of 14–70 percent to between 10 and 50 percent. The argument behind this proposal was that high marginal income tax rates discourage work and savings. This reduction would enable individuals to retain a higher percentage of the increases in income resulting from greater productivity. Greater productivity would be accompanied by an increase in production, savings, investment, and productivity, giving rise to a "virtuous circle" that would increase the tax base and thereby reduce the initial cost to the treasury of the tax reduction. It was similarly argued that this reduction would discourage the use of fiscal reliefs that shift investment toward more profitable assets from the point of view of tax relief. According to the ERP projections, this reduction would prevent federal taxes from continuing to absorb an increasing percentage of national income (see Chart 2).

The second aspect of the ERP tax proposal is the accelerated cost recovery system, which allows for speedier discounting of certain capital expenditures through simplified rules and regulations replacing the current complex system of depreciation. The proposed legislation adopted a 10-5-3 scheme for machinery and equipment used by companies and buildings occupied by the owners in industry and distribution services.[12] This system of accelerated depreciation would go into effect for assets acquired after 31 December 1980.

Monetary Policy

In the United States, the Federal Reserve, an independent agency of the executive branch, is responsible for monetary policy. The administration does not have the legal capacity to influence the course of this policy. Nevertheless, there is a margin of political pressure that the chief executive can apply to the reserve, and the activities of the Federal Reserve are partly influenced by the compatibility of their goals for monetary growth with other aspects of the overall federal economic policy, particularly the fiscal policy.

The ERP anticipated the administration's intention to preserve the independence of the Federal Reserve, exchange information on the respective policy trends, and support the reserve's decision to gradually reduce the monetary supply. As described, one essential premise of the ERP was that inflation is a purely monetary phenomenon and that it is therefore the responsibility of monetary policy to control it.

If there is a gradually progressive reduction through the years in the growth of the money supply and credit, it will be possible to

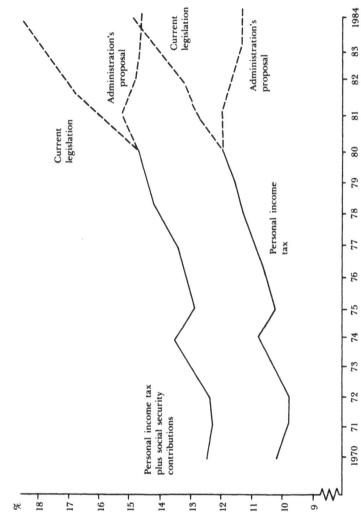

Chart 2. Personal Taxes as a Percentage of Personal Income, 1970–1984

Source: America's New Beginning: A Program for Economic Recovery, Presidential message to Congress on the occasion of the presentation of the ERP, 18 February 1981 (Washington, D.C.: GPO, 1981).

permanently and substantially reduce inflation. For this reason, the Administration supports the goal of the Federal Reserve to continue to seek a gradual reduction in the future growth of monetary aggregates and credit.[13]

In October 1979, the Federal Reserve introduced an important modification of its monetary policy. The intervention of the monetary authorities had so far been based on the establishment of objectives and an attempt to control the interest rates (especially the federal fund levels) in order to influence monetary conditions. The basic criticism of this type of operation was the difficulty in calculating the changes in the interest rates needed to steer the monetary market in the desired direction. According to this criticism, the errors in calculation gave the monetary policy a procyclical trend that increased the fluctuations in monetary aggregates as well as in the entire economy.[14] This procyclical behavior was complemented by an increase in the money stock and inflation. As this increased, the level of the interest rates became more credible as indices of the monetary policy.

At the beginning of the seventies, the Federal Reserve established monetary growth objectives while continuing to use interest rates as the principal mechanism for attaining these goals. In October 1979, this process was abandoned in favor of direct control over the amount of bank reserves, which supposedly is closely linked to the monetary supply. As a result of this new instrumentation of its monetary policy, the Federal Reserve would allow interest rates to be fixed in the market and would allow increased fluctuations.[15] As stated in the ERP, "improved monetary control is incompatible with the short-term management of interest rates. However, if the monetary policy concentrates on long-term objectives, the resulting monetary and credit restriction will interact with the tax proposals and public expenditure so as to reduce inflation and interest rates."[16]

The main change in the procedure followed by the Federal Reserve thus occurred before the new administration took over. The administration nevertheless made it known that it identified with the monetary policy as defined by the competent authority and intended to formulate policies compatible with that policy. The expected repercussions on the fiscal policy were reduced pressure for a monetization of the deficit and the provision of a future stable context to fulfill expectations. As we shall see, the administration encountered serious difficulties in keeping the commitments set forth in the ERP.

Control Policy

Control measures include provisions relating to environmental protection, health and labor security, consumer protection, and the control of certain industrial activities. These measures all provide benefits to society. According to conventional economic theory, regulation costs are channeled (1) through the maintenance costs of the agency and the bureaucracy entrusted with the administration and application of provisions; (2) through the private sector's costs for satisfying regulation requirements; and (3) through the effects of private sector costs on growth, investment, and productivity. The last two costs are extremely difficult to ascertain. Consequently, the implementation of cost/benefit analysis is dependent on the budgets devised for the two areas.[17]

The administration's view is that the sustained increase in control measures over the past years (see Chart 3) has had an adverse effect on the U.S. economy. During the first month of office, in an effort to reduce control measures, the new administration organized a task force on regulatory relief headed by Vice-President George Bush. The task force was to examine all regulations and propose necessary changes. In his first days of office, Reagan also abolished the Council on Wage and Price Stability and expedited the elimination of domestic oil price controls.

The Administration's Forecast for the ERP

The ERP constituted an important break from the traditional Keynesian economic policy that had prevailed in previous decades. It was based on the belief that economic agents make the most appropriate choices for the existing situation. A corollary to this was the belief that the best contribution the government can make is to provide a stable and foreseeable situation, allowing economic agents to plan with relative certainty for the future.

> The reduction in personal tax will allow individuals to retain a greater proportion of their earnings, thus having greater incentives to save and work. The reduction in company taxes will provide greater

Chart 3. Growth of Federal Regulatory Agencies, 1900–1980

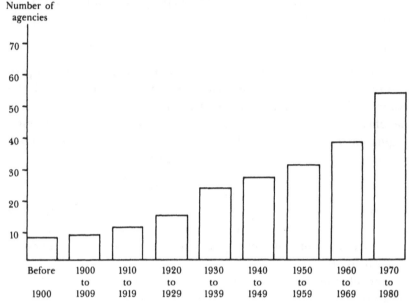

Source: Office of the President, *Economic Report of the President,* 1982 (Washington, D.C.: GPO, 1982).

incentives to raise capital, thus increasing the workers' productivity. The reduction in expenditure and the removal of unnecessary regulations would replace control over the private sector resources, where there are greater incentives for economizing. A stable monetary policy, together with an increase in productive capacity, will bring about a reduction in the rate of inflation.[18]

On the basis of these assumptions, the administration foresaw a substantial improvement in the economic indices by 1982, anticipating rapid economic growth and a reduction in unemployment and inflation. The administration also forecast a sustained reduction in the relation between expenditures, taxes, and GNP, as well as in the fiscal deficit (see Tables 5 and 6). Table 7 shows the administration's forecast.

According to the administration, the projected benefits would not materialize unless the total economic policy package was implemented.

Table 7. Economic Estimates for 1981–1986 (calendar years)

	1981	1982	1983	1984	1985	1986
Nominal GNP (billions 1972 US$)	$2,920	3,293	3,700	4,098	4,500	4,918
Percentage change	11.1	12.8	12.4	10.8	9.8	9.3
Real GNP (billions US$)	$1,497	1,560	1,638	1,711	1,783	1,858
Percentage change	1.1	4.2	5.0	4.5	4.2	4.2
Deflator of implicit prices	195	211	226	240	252	265
Percentage change	9.9	8.3	7.0	6.0	5.4	4.9
Consumer price index[a] (1967 = 100)	274	297	315	333	348	363
Percentage change	11.1	8.3	6.2	5.5	4.7	4.2
Unemployment rate (%)	7.8	7.2	6.6	6.4	6.0	5.6

[a]Consumer price index for urban workers and employees.

Source: *America's New Beginning: A Program for Economic Recovery*, Presidential message to Congress on the occasion of the presentation of the ERP, 18 February 1981 (Washington, D.C.: GPO, 1981).

The economic assumptions in this message may seem optimistic to some observers. They truly represent a dramatic break from trends in recent years. Moreover, the proposed policies constitute a new point of departure. Indeed, if each section of this broad program is quickly and fully applied, the economic panorama could improve even more rapidly than predicted by these assumptions.[19]

A factor of critical importance to the successful outcome of the ERP was the quick response of supply to tax reductions and to revised expectations. Various analysts have discussed the weakness of this operating hypothesis. In their view, exaggerated emphasis was placed on the role of relative prices (and tax reduction) as determining factors of savings, investment, and labor supply; exaggerated emphasis was placed on the beneficial effects of a reduction in the state's economic activity; and the dichotomy established between monetary and real phenomena did not adjust to reality.

Implementation of the Economic Recovery Program

The Economic Recovery Program constituted the basis of the proposal submitted to Congress by the Reagan administration in February 1981. This program was altered somewhat during legislative approval and—due to the prevailing economic situation—throughout its implementation. In this section we discuss the implementation of the ERP and its effects on the U.S. economy during 1981 and 1982.

The ERP Contradictions

As noted, the ERP contained contradictory concepts and recommendations regarding economic policy. The monetarists considered a recessive process to be practically inevitable—although its severity would depend upon expectations and the response of the affected variables (prices and salaries), but supply siders thought it feasible to support rapid economic growth while simultaneously bringing down inflation rates. In more concrete terms, the supply siders concentrated almost exclusively on the tax cut and on monetary restriction. The more conventional "old orthodoxy" insisted instead on reducing public expenditure and subsequently reducing taxes, thereby achieving a fiscal policy compatible with the monetary restriction proposal. Furthermore, there was strong pressure on the administration for a substantial increase in defense expenditure, based on national security criteria. This contradiction in priorities led to the partial inclusion of each element in the ERP (tax cuts, cuts in public expenditure other than defense, and monetary restriction), in a combination that would eventually prove untenable. In effect, the planned reduction in the growth rate of nondefense public expenditure was insufficient to compensate for the loss of fiscal income due to tax reduction, unless the hypothesis of rapid economic growth that would widen the tax base and contract the anticyclical public expenditure was confirmed. If this did not occur, the fiscal policy would cause a marked increase in the deficit, in conflict with the restrictive monetary policy that the Federal Reserve was expected to pursue. It would also create pressure for an even greater increase in the fiscal imbalance, as a result of the increase in interest payments on the public debt.

The administration was almost completely successful in obtaining legislative approval for the ERP in mid-1981. With respect to its proposals for cuts in public spending (detailed in March of 1981), the intense pressure placed on Congress by the executive encouraged their approval in August 1981 along lines similar to the proposals originally made by the administration. With minor changes, the Economic Recovery Tax Act proposed some months before by the administration was also approved in August.[20]

Based on the ERP and related measures, the approved budget for fiscal year 1982 included an expenditure level of $705 billion, income in the amount of $662 billion, and a deficit estimated at $42 billion. (The original proposal envisaged amounts of $695 billion, $650 billion, and $45 billion respectively.)

Thus, towards the second half of 1981 the Republican administration had obtained approval of the major part of its economic program. Nevertheless, the difficulties it would have to tackle during the first two years of implementation would result in adjustments both in form and content.

The Effects of the ERP on the United States' Economy

During the early stages of the new Republican administration the economy entered its second recession in little more than a year. The Council of Economic Advisors called the period between 1980 and 1981–1982 recessions "the shortest postwar recovery period." In fact, between the last quarter of 1978 and the last quarter of 1982 the real gross national product of the United States fluctuated around a clear stagnation trend (see Chart 4).

During 1981—as can be seen by Table 8—the U.S. economy performed poorly. Although the growth rate of the real gross national product exceeded that originally foreseen by U.S. official analysts, its evolution was extremely unstable, just as it had been in 1980. Similarly, during the second and fourth quarters of the year, negative growth was recorded. During 1982 the real gross national product shrank to an annual rate of −1.8 percent. This prolonged period of stagnation lowered the levels of real production in comparison with those of 1979.

Table 8 presents data on the evolution and sectorial performance of increased demand over the two-year period. Poor economic performance in 1981 was related to the slow growth of consumer

26

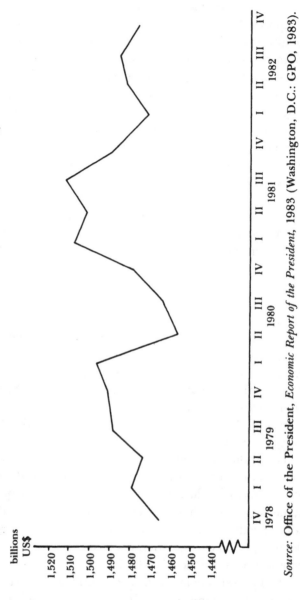

Chart 4. Evolution of the Real Gross National Product (in billions 1972 US$)

Source: Office of the President, *Economic Report of the President,* 1983 (Washington, D.C.: GPO, 1983).

Table 8. Performance of Overall Demand, 1981 and 1982 (annual growth rates, %)

	1981					1980, IV to 1981, IV	1982					1981, IV to 1982, IV
	Year	I	II	III	IV		Year	I	II	III	IV	
Consumer spending	1.8	4.3	-2.7	2.9	-3.4	0.2	1.0	2.4	2.5	0.5	4.9	2.6
Durables	2.1	16.6	-18.4	10.4	-22.8	-3.9	-0.9	10.1	2.3	-5.5	18.8	6.5
Nondurables	1.8	2.9	0.1	1.4	0.1	1.1	0.8	-1.0	2.5	1.5	2.5	1.4
Services	1.7	1.5	0.1	1.7	0	0.8	1.8	2.9	2.4	1.6	2.6	2.4
Fixed private investment	1.7	6.1	-3.3	-0.9	-5.2	-0.8	-5.3	-6.2	-7.8	-7.4	-3.2	-6.0
Nonhousing	3.5	7.9	0.9	8.9	0.7	4.7	-3.8	-5.1	-12.3	-7.9	-9.3	-8.4
Housing	-4.9	0.8	-18.5	-37.2	-30.0	19.4	-10.9	10.0	12.3	-6.0	22.3	4.5
Govt. expend. (goods & serv.)	0.9	5.1	-4.0	3.5	6.8	2.9	1.4	-2.9	-5.4	8.1	10.8	2.6
Defense	4.9	8.0	10.7	7.7	9.7	9.3	7.1	-8.4	19.9	12.3	3.5	6.8
Nondefense	1.0	4.3	-9.1	2.3	5.6	0.7	-0.5	-0.9	-14.2	6.4	14.1	1.2
Final domestic demand	1.6	4.7	-3.1	2.4	-1.5	0.6	0.1	0.1	-0.6	0.9	5.0	1.3
Inventory changes[a]	0.9	2.3	2.6	1.2	-3.1	0.7	-1.2	-5.4	3.0	2.1	-5.7	-1.5
Total domestic demand	2.6	7.1	-0.4	3.6	-4.6	1.4	-1.2	-5.5	2.5	3.1	-0.9	-0.2
Exports of goods & serv.	-0.4	10.8	1.0	-4.8	-2.3	1.2	-6.9	-13.3	7.1	-17.9	-30.1	-13.1
Imports of goods & serv.	7.2	5.5	15.8	11.1	5.7	9.8	0.7	-18.9	13.9	4.4	-15.7	-4.2
External balance[a]	-0.6	0.7	-1.1	-1.3	-0.7	-0.6	-0.8	—	-0.1	-0.6	-0.4	-1.0
Gross national product	1.9	7.9	-1.5	2.2	-5.3	0.7	-1.8	-5.2	2.1	0.7	-2.5	-1.2

[a]The changes are expressed as a percentage of the GNP of the previous period.

Source: Office of the President, Economic Report of the President, 1983 (Washington, D.C.: GPO, 1983).

spending (with a reduction in the durable goods component), the reduction in fixed private investment (especially housing investment, which was hard hit by financial conditions), and the negative influence of the external sector. During 1982 the fundamental determinants of the situation were the liquidation of inventories and the reduction in net exports. Fixed investment also dropped, although in 1982 the reduction was in nonhousing investment.

The evolution of the external sector played a very important role. The effects of the international recession and the strengthening of the dollar (see Table 9) had a marked depressive influence on the U.S. economy. Table 10 shows the quarterly evolution of U.S. exports and imports. This negative macroeconomic performance had an immediate effect on the labor market. During the last quarter of 1981 the unemployment rate rose to 8.3 percent. As the trend continued, unemployment reached 10.7 percent in the same period of the following year, the highest rate in almost fifty years (see Table 11). Towards the end of 1982 the number of persons employed was less than in 1980. The number employed in the manufacturing sector had dropped by 10 percent.

The depressed state of the labor market undoubtedly had a significant effect on the behavior of nominal salaries (Table 12). Throughout 1981, and particularly in 1982, salaries showed significantly restrained growth, laying the basis for a decrease in the inflation rate. During 1982, real salaries (measured by the indicators shown in Table 12) increased for the first time over a five-year period, as a result of the rapid reduction in inflation. The more unionized sectors and regions were hardest hit by the reduction in demand (steel, automotive, and construction industries), and their role in fixing nominal salaries quickly affected the rest of the labor market.

The economic policy of the Reagan administration has undoubtedly been decisive in shaping the development of the U.S. economy in the last few years. The most serious problem faced by the macroeconomic policy has been the coexistence of contradictory instruments and mutually exclusive objectives. While the monetary policy attempted to control inflation by restricting circulation, the fiscal policy became expansive as a result of the reduction in taxes and the increase in military expenditure, which was inadequately compensated by a reduction in the growth rate of social expenditure.

Table 9. Relative Value of the U.S. Dollar, 1980–1982 (March 1973 index = 100)[a]

Year	Nominal	Real[b]
1980	87.4	84.8
1981	102.9	100.8
I	94.5	92.3
II	103.1	100.3
III	110.0	108.0
IV	105.4	102.7
1982	116.6	111.7
I	109.9	106.0
II	114.0	109.2
III	119.3	115.3
IV	122.2	116.2

[a]Weighted in accordance with the participation of the principal trading partners.
[b]Deflated by the urban consumer price index.

Source: Office of the President, Economic Report of the President, 1983 (Washington, D.C.: GPO, 1983).

Table 10. Annual Growth Rate of U.S. Exports and Imports of Goods, 1981 and 1982 (%)

	1981				1982		
	I	II	III	IV	I	II	III
Total exports	19.5	−2.6	−17.2	−0.7	−12.6	−4.3	−19.5
Total imports	12.4	11.3	−7.7	−7.6	−30.7	−5.1	26.7
Nonoil imports	11.2	14.1	11.7	11.0	−53.9	−57.1	90.5

Source: Office of the President, Economic Report of the President, 1983 (Washington, D.C.: GPO, 1983).

The main consequences of the strict monetary policy were the recessive process just described and the significant increase and variability of nominal and real interest rates. The severity of the recession quickly reduced inflationary pressures, which meant that real interest rates would remain significantly high. High interest

Table 11. U.S. Employment and Unemployment Rate, 1980–1982

Year	Unemployment Rate (%)	Total Employed (thousands)	Total Unemployed (thousands)	Total Employed in Manufacturing (thousands)
1980	7.1	99,303	7,637	20,285
1981	7.6	100,397	8,273	20,173
I	7.4	100,204	8,016	20,172
II	7.4	100,789	8,013	20,313
III	7.4	100,520	8,059	20,319
IV	8.3	100,087	9,029	19,892
1982	9.7	99,526	11,839	18,849
I	8.8	99,660	10,678	19,430
II	9.4	99,720	9,632	19,071
III	10.0	99,605	10,362	18,686
IV	10.7	99,135	11,025	18,214

Source: Office of the President, *Economic Report of the President*, 1983 (Washington, D.C.: GPO, 1983).

Table 12. Growth Rate of Income and Prices, 1980–1982 (%)

	1980	1981	1982
Average hourly income index (annual growth rate)	9.0	9.1	6.8
Hourly rate	10.2	9.7	7.2
Productivity	−0.9	1.4	0.1
Unit costs	11.2	8.1	7.0
GNP Deflator	9.3	9.4	6.0
Consumer price index	13.5	10.4	6.1
Average hourly real income	−4.5	−1.3	0.7
Real hourly rate	−3.3	−0.7	1.1

Source: Office of the President, *Economic Report of the President*, 1983 (Washington, D.C.: GPO, 1983).

rates were probably also related to uncertain future prospects linked to the expected size of fiscal deficits.

A summary of monetary sector data for 1981 and 1982 is presented in Table 13. This table shows "real" interest rates, calculated by deflating the nominal increase in the consumer price index during the period. The adjustment involved is an extremely rough one, but it does give an indication of the general trend.

During the period in question, interest rates and the monetary stock fluctuated considerably, although up to the second half of 1982 a clear contraction trend was evident. The increase in the second half of 1982 was interpreted by official analysts as a result of changes in the financial system (greater search for liquidity) and accompanying trends (the maturing of the All-Savers Certificates within the last quarter of the year). Based on these arguments, the monetary authorities pointed out that the Federal Reserve would not necessarily aim to achieve their monetary growth objectives (fixed within a 2.5–5.5 percent range) in the second half of the year. At the same time, the budgetary resolution passed by Congress in June 1982 indicated a general feeling in that body that the Federal Reserve Board "will have to reassess its monetary goals, to ensure that they are absolutely compatible with a new and more restrictive policy."

In fact, 1982 clearly revealed the conflict between the monetary and the fiscal policy of the Republican administration. During that fiscal year, the deficit originally predicted at $42 billion reached $110 billion. Within the context of a restrictive monetary policy, this fiscal imbalance undoubtedly had a profound effect on the economy. Public sector financing had attracted an average of 19 percent of the total funds on the credit market during the 1975–1979 period; during 1982 this percentage rose to almost 34 percent (Table 14).

The source of the budgetary imbalance was the Economic Recovery Tax Act (ERTA) passed in 1981, which caused a substantial reduction in the treasury's tax-derived income. According to the Budget Office of Congress, the reductions approved in 1981 imply a reduction in federal income equivalent to 3.9 percent of the GNP for the fiscal year 1984, and 5.6 percent in 1988. This reduction in fiscal revenue was not accompanied by a comparable cut in federal spending. On the contrary, public expenditure increased in

Table 13. Monetary Stock and Interest Rates, 1980–1982 (%)

	1980	1981					1982				
		Year	I	II	III	IV	Year	I	II	III	IV
M$_1$ (growth rate)[a]	6.6	6.4	3.5	9.2	0.3	5.7	8.2	10.4	3.3	3.4	16.1
M$_1$ (growth rate)	8.4[b]	4.7[b]					8.5[b]				
Three-month treasury bills	11.5	14.1	14.4	14.8	15.1	12.1	10.7	12.9	12.4	9.7	7.9
Aaa corporate bonds	11.9	14.2	13.2	14.0	14.0	14.6	13.8	15.0	14.5	13.7	11.9
Prime rate	15.3	18.9	20.2	19.7	20.5	17.7	14.9	16.4	16.5	15.2	12.3
CPI (growth rate)[c]	13.5	10.4	9.6	7.6	12.0	5.2	6.1	1.2	10.8	3.6	−1.2
Three-month treasury bills, "real"[d]	−2.0	3.7	4.8	7.2	3.1	6.8	4.5	11.7	1.6	6.1	9.1
Aaa corporate bonds, "real"	−1.6	3.8	3.6	6.4	2.9	9.4	7.7	13.8	3.7	7.6	13.1
Prime rate, "real"	1.8	8.5	10.6	12.1	8.5	12.5	8.8	15.2	5.7	11.6	13.5

[a]M$_1$ = monetary aggregate.
[b]Fourth quarter to fourth quarter.
[c]CPI = consumer price index
[d]"real" = nominal deflated by CPI

Source: Office of the President, *Economic Report of the President,* 1983 (Washington, D.C.: GPO, 1983).

Table 14. Funds Attracted on Credit Markets by the Nonfinancial Sector, 1975–1982 (%)

	1975–79	1980	1981	1982
U.S. government	18.6	19.9	21.5	33.6
External sector	6.1	7.4	6.7	2.7
Domestic nonfinancial private sector	75.3	72.7	71.8	63.7
Total	100.0	100.0	100.0	100.0

Source: Office of the President, Economic Report of the President, 1983 (Washington, D.C.: GPO, 1983).

absolute terms and as a percentage of the GNP. The main components of the increase were defense expenditure, with an estimated annual growth of 7 percent in real terms for the 1983–1988 period; interest payments on public debt; and nondiscriminatory social programs such as social security, Medicaid and Medicare, and food stamps. According to these estimates, federal expenditure in 1988 will represent 24 percent of the GNP, while fiscal revenue will shrink to 18 percent, creating a deficit of 6 percent.

This disproportion between federal expenditure and income has fueled an increasing deficit containing a significant structural component. According to the Budget Office of Congress, approximately two-thirds of the current deficit reflects the reaction to a weakened economy; this leaves approximately $70 billion worth of structural deficit. Because this deficit is not expected to decrease in the future—as is usually the case in recoveries—it has become a focal point of discussion. It is appropriate to recall that in August 1982 Congress passed new tax legislation (the Tax Equity and Fiscal Responsibility Act) that reversed approximately 65 percent of the tax concessions granted to corporations a year before, and 10 percent of individual concessions. Even so, the imbalance will continue into the future.

Table 15 lists several estimates of the "high employment deficit" in the future. These figures are based on the assumption that the economy is operating at a 6 percent level of unemployment. The deficits show a generally high and upward trend, particularly if one assumes that there will be no change in policy (first two lines). The rapid growth in the deficit after 1985 reflects the indexing of the tax base from 1 January 1985, incorporated in the 1981 ERTA.

This persistent fiscal imbalance in the United States promises a future crisis of proportions equal to the crisis of the last two years. The actual deficits of fiscal years 1981, 1982, and 1983 and the deficit anticipated for 1984 (Table 16) can be compared with the original projections of the ERP presented in Table 5.

In short, during its first two years of implementation (1981–1982), the ERP has caused a severe recession, increased unemployment, a drop in absolute levels of employment, and a reduction in inflationary trends. It has created a pronounced imbalance in federal public accounts, projected to continue in the future. In conjunction with the restrictive monetary policy implemented by the Federal Reserve, the ERP has also encouraged a marked increase and variability in nominal and real interest rates. Furthermore, as the implementation of the monetary policy excluded participation in exchange markets, fluctuations in interest rates have had a destabilizing influence on currency quotations.

Recent Changes and Prospects in U.S. Economic Policy

As anticipated, the ERP underwent several changes in form and content in the course of implementation. The process of readjustment has accelerated dramatically in recent months as a result of the pressure exerted by national and international events. In mid-1982 the national economic picture was extremely serious, as evidenced by prolonged productive stagnation, the highest unemployment levels in four decades, and extremely uncertain prospects. Likewise, public finances seemed to be out of control, and an overwhelming burden of massive deficits seemed likely in the future. Within the context of a depressed market, monetary restriction and high financial burdens had caused the highest number of bankruptcies recorded since 1933. These occurred not only among small and medium-sized firms, but also among large corporations and in the financial sector.

In August 1982, the Tax Equity and Fiscal Responsibility Act was passed to ensure an increase of almost $100 billion in taxes for the next three-year period. This measure represented a step backward from the tax program passed the year before, although

Table 15. Projection of the "High Employment Deficit," Fiscal Years 1982–1988 (billions US$)

	1982	1983	1984	1985	1986	1987	1988
Without policy changes							
Congressional Budget Office (CBO)[a]	23	72	96	125	155	187	218
Center for National Policy[a]	na	70	100	125	155	185	220
With policy changes							
CBO base projection with the administration's proposals for reduction in expenditure	na	72	71	91	72	97	106
Data Resources Inc. (DRI)[b]	45	74	82	85	83	71	59

[a]In defining high employment, the Budget Office and the Center for National Policy assume a 6 percent unemployment rate.
[b]In defining high employment, DRI assumes a 6 percent unemployment rate. Policy changes go beyond the reductions proposed by the administration and include a tax increase.

Sources: Central Budgetary Office, *An Analysis of the President's Budgetary Proposals for Fiscal Year 1984,* February 1983, I, II-2; Data Resources Inc., *US Review,* February 1983, p. 1.39, Table 2; Walter Heller, "Introduction," *Budget and Policy Choices 1983: Taxes, Defense, Entitlements* (Washington, D.C.: Center for National Policy, 1983), p. 9.

Table 16. Federal Income, Expenditure, and Deficit, 1980–1984

	1980	1981	1982	1983	1984[a]
Income	517,112	599,272	617,766	597,494	659,702
Expenditure	576,675	657,204	728,375	805,202	848,483
Deficit (−) or surplus (+)	−59,563	−57,932	−110,609	−207,708	−188,781

[a]Projected.

Source: Office of the President, *Economic Report of the President,* 1983 (Washington, D.C.: GPO, 1983).

the administration insisted on presenting it otherwise. However, this measure did not solve the crux of the matter—the structural imbalance in public accounts. In February 1983, the president submitted his budgetary proposal for the fiscal year 1984, reaffirming his well-known priorities of increased defense expenditure and cuts in social expenditure. In more concrete terms, the proposal recommends freezing the total amount of real public expenditure, increasing military expenditure by 10 percent in real terms, and approving a standby tax for a three-year period as of 1985. The tax will be implemented provided that first, the program's measures related to expenditure are passed, and second, that the deficit exceeds 2.5 percent of the GNP in 1985. At the time of writing, this proposal is being discussed in Congress. Apparently, the "consensus" being reached in Congress includes a reduction in planned defense expenditure, a decrease in other domestic expenditure (particularly for the more extensive programs such as social security), and eventually an increase in taxes—or at least the elimination of indexing, scheduled to govern income tax as of 1 January 1985. Despite all this, there is little likelihood of the fiscal imbalance disappearing in the near future.

Monetary policy is also being redefined. Since the second half of 1982, the Federal Reserve has progressively reduced the discount rate and allowed a larger increase in bank reserves and in the money supply than they originally foresaw. Everything seems to indicate that this "flexibility" will continue in the immediate future. Paul Volcker, president of the Board of Governors of the Federal Reserve, who was reappointed in June 1983 for a new term, has persistently indicated his decision "to support the present recovery." However, in spite of these efforts, the reduction in interest rates has been less than expected, at least in proportion to the reduction in the discount rate. In this respect, the role played by the large fiscal deficits predicted for the future is very significant, particularly with regard to the behavior of long-term interest rates. The likelihood that demands for public sector financing will again place pressure on future monetary policy is still affecting the market.

These changes in the economic policy orientation of the Republican administration coincide with the apparent beginning of a recovery in the first quarter of 1983. According to official projections, real economic growth will reach 1.4 percent during 1983 (about 4 percent, if one compares the fourth quarter of 1983 with that of 1982), and will exceed 4 percent after 1984. Based on these projections, the administration expects an average unemployment rate of 10.7 percent for 1983, falling to 7.4 percent in 1987. The duration of existing conditions in the labor market may affect the reduction trend in inflationary pressures.

However, the 1983 recovery raises many questions. In fact, the projections of the administration itself indicate a performance level far below the historical average recorded in every other postwar recovery. Some analysts calculate that the United States' trade deficit for 1983 will be approximately $70 billion. In addition to its depressive effect on overall demand, such a significant increase in the external imbalance could dramatically affect the relative value of the dollar and introduce new elements of instability into the already precarious international monetary situation.

Other factors that cast doubt on the economic recovery are its slow pace and the economy's real performance during the first quarter of 1983. The slow pace forecast for the development of economic activity will likely mean continued high levels of idle capacity and consequently, little incentive to investment. And if there is no increase in investment, the current improvement is unlikely to persist. Furthermore, information on the first quarter of 1983 indicates that the change in economic performance is fundamentally due to a decrease in the rate of working off inventories in comparison to the final quarter of 1982. Economic activity has also been positively affected by the construction sector, which has been bolstered by a reduction in mortgage interest rates and by recent signs of recovery from the extreme depression that has undermined the industry over the past few years. Consumer expenditure, however, has been ineffectual, and nonhousing private investment continued to contract in 1983. According to a survey conducted by the Department of Commerce in 1983, capital expenditure in the corporate sector will decline by 5.2 percent in real terms in comparison to the previous year. Nevertheless, recent months have offered new signs of an economic revival, although its intensity and scope are still debatable.

Notes

1. Office of the President, *Economic Report of the President*, 1972 (Washington, D.C.: GPO, 1972), p. 5.

2. *America's New Beginning: A Program for Economic Recovery*, Presidential message to Congress on the occasion of the presentation of the ERP, 18 February 1981 (Washington, D.C.: GPO, 1981), p. 2.

3. By quarters, the actual gross national product grew at the following annual rates: first quarter, 3.1 percent; second quarter, −9.9 percent; third quarter, 2.4 percent; and fourth quarter, 3.8 percent. The drop in real production during the second quarter of the year was the largest in the entire postwar period, exceeding even the decline recorded in the worst quarter of 1975.

4. This increase in the inflation rate was not only a function of oil price increases in 1979. Apart from the cost of energy, food, and the purchase and financing of housing, the consumer price index rose from an annual rate of 7.3 percent in 1979 to 9.0 percent in 1980.

5. The "high employment budget deficit" dropped from $−23 billion in 1977 to $−15 billion in 1978 and $−2.2 billion in 1979.

6. During the final quarter of 1979, savings reached their lowest level in twenty-eight years: 4.7 percent of disposable income.

7. Office of the President, *Economic Report of the President*, 1982 (Washington, D.C.: GPO, 1982), p. 21.

8. M. Friedman, *Unemployment Versus Inflation*, Institute of Economic Affairs Occasional Paper no. 44, 1975; E. S. Phelps, "Phillips Curves, Expectations of Inflation and Optimal Unemployment over Time," *Economica*, August 1967.

9. *Economic Report of the President*, 1982, p. 52.

10. Ibid., p. 27.

11. *America's New Beginning*.

12. The assets with an amortization period of three years are cars, light-duty trucks, and equipment and machinery used for research and development (these will also enjoy a 6 percent tax credit). All other types of machinery and equipment up to eighteen years old in 1981 would be deductible in five years (this category will also receive a 10 percent tax credit). Production premises, warehouses, and sales offices used by the owners with a current depreciation rate exceeding eighteen years would be deducted in ten years.

13. *America's New Beginning*, p. 22.

14. According to this interpretation, a vigorous demand for credit increased the market interest rate, making monetary policy seem restrictive.

This was followed by greater flexibility, which led to an excessive increase in liquidity. The opposite occurred in periods of depressed liquidity and credit demand. See *Economic Report of the President*, 1982, p. 66.

15. The control variable would be the bank reserves, which may affect the Federal Reserve through loan operations at the discount window of the central bank. The Federal Reserve is forced to make loans available in its capacity as "last resort lender." However, reserves taken in loans normally represent a small percentage of total reserves, so a significant influence was not expected on the money supply.

16. *America's New Beginning*, p. 23.

17. The regulation of certain U.S. industrial sectors is frequently referred to as a cause of their deterioration and loss of competitive ability. For example, during the seventies, the U.S. steel industry spent an average of $365 million to reduce pollution and safeguard workers' security. This amount represented about 17 percent of the sector's total investment for the decade. However, 48 percent was subscribed by the state and municipal governments in industrial development bonds. Moreover, Japanese steel producers spent more than double that amount for the same period. More than the total amount of expenditure, the decisive element appears to be the economic dynamism that makes the regulatory cost more or less conflicting. See Robert Reich, "The Formulation of Industrial Policy," *Cuadernos Semestrales* 13, IEEU-CIDE (Instituto de Estudios de Estados Unidos–Centro de Investigación y Docencia Económicas), Semester 1, 1983.

18. *America's New Beginning*, p. 24.

19. Ibid., p. 25.

20. The amendments were: (1) marginal personal tax rates would be reduced by 25 percent within three years—5 percent in 1981, 10 percent in 1982, and 10 percent in 1983; (2) income would be indexed in relation to the income tax collected from 1 January 1985 (this measure was intended to eliminate the "inflation tax" that resulted from higher fiscal incomes caused by the inflationary process and the corresponding increases in personal income); (3) reduction of the windfall profits tax on certain oil-producing wells, authorization to "transfer" gains derived from the system of accelerated depreciation from businesses without profits to others showing profits, and other minor changes.

2

U.S. International
Economic Policy

Principles of the Reagan Administration's
International Economic Policy

Within the original framework of the Republican administration, international economic policy was relegated to a secondary position, in sharp contrast with the relatively intense and systematic attention paid to it by the preceding Democratic administration. The Carter administration had formulated initiatives toward improving coordination among the economic policies of industrialized countries and had begun negotiations to meet the demands of developing countries.

The Republican administration's treatment of international economic issues was largely influenced by its foreign policy priorities, which concentrated on recovering a dominant position in U.S. relations with the Soviet Union and establishing decisive U.S. leadership among its allies. Within this framework, preference was given to the adoption of a firm, imposing attitude rather than to negotiation. This position reflected the basic assumption that the deterioration in U.S. hegemony (military, political, and economic) was due to the leadership's lack of resolve and credibility rather than to the development of tendencies intrinsic to the evolution of the international system.

The new administration's attitude toward international economic problems was partly shaped by the view that the less the market was interfered with and the longer trade liberalization and global interaction continued, the more positive would be the results. The administration also emphasized that errors in managing the domestic economic policy of each nation were the prime determinants of international economic imbalances. Based on these considerations, the central principles governing the international economic policy of the Reagan administration in its initial stages can be summarized as follows.

The Privilege of Security

The subjection of economic problems and conflicts to the rationale of East-West confrontation and the use of security criteria have been the basic factors determining the orientation and content of the administration's international economic policy. In the words of Secretary of State Alexander Haig, "the need to promote and protect our security will be the prime determining factor in formulating economic policy, in allocating our resources and in deciding on international economic issues."[1]

It is not surprising that the principles governing the administration's international economic policy fall within the strategic globalism that also informs its perspective on foreign policy and international relations. Coordination and negotiation take second place to the reaffirmation of U.S. interests and unilateral "leadership." Bilateralism is also regaining importance vis-à-vis multilateralism; it is considered a more effective mechanism to promote the United States' political and security interests through its international economic policy.

During the first half of the administration's term of office, this concern for security issues permeated U.S. external economic relations with the socialist bloc, with industrialized countries, and with the developing world. The restriction on the transfer of U.S. technology for the construction of the Siberian pipeline is an example of how these issues have affected relations with the socialist bloc and with the country's industrialized allies as well. Washington's decision to sanction Moscow had a high political cost in its relations with other industrialized countries. Paradoxically, the U.S. action transformed a sanction aimed against the USSR into an essentially U.S.-European problem. It demonstrated the Reagan administration's conviction that the United States still has sufficient power to impose actions and policy decisions on its European allies with no consideration for consensus nor for uniform national interest. The changes and content of foreign aid programs also clearly indicate how security criteria and the emphasis on East-West conflict have influenced the conduct of relations with developing countries.

Emphasis on the Market and the Private Sector

The second directional principle of the Reagan administration's international economic policy is its emphasis on the role of the private sector and market mechanisms in international economic relations. The administration has adopted at the international level the same criteria it applied to the domestic economy. In the administration's view, the market is the ideal mechanism to achieve satisfactory economic results, and emphasis should therefore be placed on removing obstacles that prevent the free operation of the market. Because the private sector forms the basis for commercial relations, the government should encourage it to assume increasing responsibility in managing international economic activities.

"We do not believe that greater economic prosperity for all countries in the world will result from agreements formulated by negotiating teams discussing the meaning of abstract terms, but rather from an open international system which will provide a framework beneficial to international cooperation with respect to specific problems."[2] Reiterating ideas he had already expounded in presenting his domestic economic program, President Reagan declared to the joint IMF–World Bank meeting in September 1981: "The societies which have achieved the most spectacular and far-reaching economic progress in the shortest period of time are those which believe in the magic of the market."[3]

The administration's emphasis on the fostering of private capital flows by multilateral financial organizations is one clear indication of the consequences of this position. Its support for broadening the activities of the International Finance Corporation and for cofinancing agreements are other examples.

The Primacy of Internal Reorganization

Finally, a third basic principle of the Reagan administration's international economic policy is the key role assigned to recovery and internal reorganization of every nation's economy in restoring favorable conditions at the international level. At the joint meeting of the IMF and the World Bank, President Reagan pointed out:

> The most important contribution a country can make to international development is the pursuing of healthy domestic policies. Unfortunately, last year many industrialized countries, including my own, did not make this contribution. We have exceeded spending limits, we have increased tax levels too high and have been excessive in our regulatory measures. As a result, we are faced today with slow growth and increasing inflation.[4]

In the light of this, the main responsibility of the United States was "to put its house in order" within the guidelines and principles discussed in the previous chapter. Although in the short term this could be a traumatic process, in the medium and long term it will create the right conditions for sustained and stable international economic growth. This is how, the administration reasoned, implementing the ERP would influence the entire international economy.[5]

Trade Policy

The general principles just described have a specific application in U.S. trade and investment policy. However, the actual conditions of the domestic and international economy have influenced their concrete application.

In the area of trade, the Reagan administration adopted the traditional postwar position, favoring an open trade system as representing the most effective way of increasing international well-being. In July 1981, the new government made public its official position in its *Statement on U.S. Trade Policy*, which included five focal points:

1. The restoration of noninflationary domestic growth in order to improve the ability of U.S. companies to respond to changes

in the domestic and international markets. A dynamic internal atmosphere makes the domestic economy more competitive, while creating an expanding labor market that facilitates the adjustment of those sectors displaced by international competition.

2. The reduction of trade barriers inherent in complex trade legislation and of regulatory measures that inhibit exports and imports.

3. The effective and strict application of U.S. trade legislation and international agreements that protect free trade and regulate the application of control measures.

4. The adoption of a more effective approach to problems caused by industrial adjustment, acknowledging the role of the market as the most efficient mechanism to promote and apply adjustment.

5. The reduction of trade and investment barriers through international negotiation, particularly in the services and investment areas.

By and large, these guidelines coincide with the more general principles of international economic policy formulated by the Reagan administration. Pursuant to these recommendations, the administration began to develop a series of measures to promote and facilitate exports. Perhaps the most significant step in this direction was the approval by Congress and by the president of a bill authorizing the creation of export trading companies. The export trading companies will administer sales, marketing activities, and to a large extent, the financing of exports, stimulating the participation of small and medium enterprises that lack the resources to initiate overseas sales programs on their own.

Eximbank's decision to extend its terms of export credit to fifteen, twenty, or more years was also an important step. According to the prevailing consensus among the member countries of the Organization for Economic Cooperation and Development (OECD), the maximum period on export credits should be ten years. Eximbank's decision to the contrary continues a prolonged conflict over the appropriate level of preferential interest rates for state financing of exports from industrialized countries.

To encourage the flow of private investment and thereby stimulate the development process, the administration established a new office, the Bureau for Private Enterprise, within the Agency for International Development (AID). It also launched a series of measures aimed at strengthening the Overseas Private Investment Corporation, an organization that insures U.S. companies against expropriation and exchange risk overseas. In December 1981 a program to establish bilateral investment treaties (BITs) was launched. Its goal is "the establishment of a context favorable to the flow of private capital to developing countries."[6] Following the model proposed by the United States, a BIT normally includes four main points:

> Each government shall maintain a climate favorable to local investment by national or foreign companies and shall apply regulations and other measures in such fashion as to allow for such investment to be made on terms no less favorable than those enjoyed by its nationals or third countries, whichever is more favorable. . . . Each government shall also reserve the right to a limited number of exceptions to this pattern of treatment. . . .
>
> The expropriation or nationalization of an investment cannot occur unless it be for public purposes, following an adequate nondiscriminatory legal procedure, and accompanied by rapid, adequate and effective compensation. . . .
>
> The rights of investors to execute freely and expeditiously all transfers relating to investment in and out of the host country shall be safeguarded. . . .
>
> Preference shall be given to consultation and negotiation as the mechanism for the settlement of conflicts. This shall be done in accordance with the terms of agreement of the investment and the domestic and international legislation in force or shall be submitted to the International Centre for Settlements.[7]

Public officials are of the opinion that "by designing a common legal frame of reference for both parties, bilateral investment treaties commit both signatories to providing equitable treatment to investors, thus helping to create a more attractive climate for investment. In the 1980s, this will depend on the economic and political climate of beneficiary countries as well as on any other variable."[8]

International Action

The United States' position on the reduction of trade and international investment barriers by negotiation was clearly expressed at the General Agreement on Tariffs and Trade (GATT) meeting held in November 1982. The main points discussed there included (1) the formulation of regulations for "safeguard mechanisms"; (2) subsidies; and (3) the regulation and liberalization of trade in the services sector. With regard to the first point, the United States stressed the need to set specific limits on import restrictions that may be applied according to the safeguard measures provided for in GATT. These measures are not clearly defined, which has led to their proliferation and permanence. The United States has also made ample use of these provisions. On the second point—subsidies—the conflict between the interests of the United States and the European Economic Community (EEC) was clear. The United States tried to apply intense pressure on the Common Market countries to make the subsidy mechanisms for agricultural exports more flexible. Washington's view is that these mechanisms not only close the European market to U.S. exports but also displace U.S. products in third markets. U.S. pressure for the freeing of agricultural trade—not only in Western Europe but also in Japan—is closely linked to the dynamic role agricultural exports have played as a positive factor in the United States' trade balance in the past decade.

The third matter—the regulation and liberalization of trade in services—is a long-term concern of the United States. GATT provisions do not cover trade in services, which has greatly increased in recent decades. Moreover, the United States enjoys substantial comparative advantages in this sector; approximately two-thirds of U.S. GNP comes from the services trade. The resulting increase of external surpluses has served to compensate, in part, for the deficit trend in the trade of goods. The issue of foreign investment is closely linked to developments in the services sector. The United States has systematically opposed regulations governing foreign investments, particularly the export requirements that many developing countries apply to transnational investment for balance-of-payments and industrial policy purposes.

The 1982 Geneva GATT meeting achieved little amidst increasing trade conflicts. Meanwhile, the United States launched an important

Table 17. Structure of the U.S. Balance of Payments as a Percentage of GNP, 1960–1980

	Percentage of GNP		Percentage Change
	1960–1966	1974–1980	
Trade in goods	0.86	−0.80	−1.66
Investment-derived income	0.74	1.06	0.32
Military transactions	−0.41	−0.03	0.38
Travel and services	−0.04	0.12	0.16
Transfers	−0.44	−0.30	0.14
Current account	0.70	0.06	−0.64

Source: Office of the President, Economic Report of the President, 1983 (Washington, D.C.: GPO, 1983), p. 55.

offensive, accusing its European trading counterparts and Japan of increasing protectionism. However, this emphasis on free trade contradicts the specific practice of U.S. trade policy during the past two years. It is therefore important to comment on this policy and on the increasing pressure for the adoption of a tougher protectionist stance by the U.S. government.

Protectionism in the United States

The pressures confronting the United States' foreign trade are the combined result of long-term trends towards the structural adjustments of the U.S. economy and the difficulties associated with recession and slow growth. The industrial superiority of the U.S. economy after the Second World War declined progressively throughout subsequent decades: from the early fifties to the late seventies, the U.S. share in the world market for manufactured goods dropped by 55 percent. This decline was linked to the rapid expansion experienced first by the industrial apparatus of European countries and Japan, and subsequently by that of the newly industrialized countries (NICs). However, the decisive elements of the U.S. industrial decline were the relative stagnation of the U.S. economy and the role played by U.S. overseas investment.

The failing competitiveness of the U.S. economy is clearly reflected in its performance in foreign trade. The balance of trade in goods has tended to decrease (Table 17), but the effects on the current account have been partially offset by the favorable increase in net income from investment, services, unilateral transfers, and military transactions. This change in the structure of the United States' current account balance, which has been of paramount importance to the U.S. economy, reveals structural tendencies in its productive apparatus.

Some studies indicate that the loss in competitiveness in the U.S. economy not only affects traditional sectors such as the steel, textile, garment, footwear, electrical appliances, and more recently, the automotive industries, but also frontier and high technology activities. The majority of industrialized countries formulate more or less explicit industrial policies aimed at promoting the development of high technology products. This has accelerated the development of this sector of their economies, partly to the detriment of the United States' traditional comparative advantage. U.S. imports of high technology products, as a proportion of U.S. apparent consumption, have been increasing over the past years. In the high technology field, import levels have increased more rapidly than export levels (see Table 18).

Over the past three years, these long-term developments have been accompanied by stagnating production and a consequent increase in unemployment rates. This has increased the visibility of imports as a cause of the imbalance in U.S. production. However, the high idle capacity level in the steel or automotive industries, for example, is due not only to import pressure but also to the fall in aggregate demand and the overall level of activity. Persistent stagnation reduces the chances of making the necessary structural adjustments at the lowest possible cost.[9] Hence the increasing protectionist pressures and the resurgence of various options of industrial policy as a way of dealing with the drop in U.S. production.

Protectionism by Country

In these circumstances, the prevailing trend in the United States has been to combine a generally free trade reasoning approach with the application of selective protectionist pressures by country and by sector. This policy was accompanied in the seventies by an increase in the "new protectionism." The prolonged debate on trade policy in the United States forms part of a broader question

Table 18. U.S. Indices of High-Technology Products, 1974–1981[a]

	Proportion of Total Manufactured Goods (%)			Export Surplus in Relation to Total Exports (%)	Percentage of Imports in Apparent Consumption[b]
Year	Deliveries	Exports	Imports		
1974	13.2	29.3	13.0	55.8	8.3
1975	12.5	28.3	14.0	59.6	8.0
1976	12.5	28.9	16.2	49.8	9.5
1977	12.4	29.3	15.8	45.7	9.5
1978	12.8	30.3	16.5	42.0	10.9
1979	13.3	30.0	16.3	47.7	10.5
1980	14.2	31.5	17.5	50.3	11.2
1981	13.9	32.2	18.8	45.0	11.9

[a]Trade computed on Standard Industrial Classification (SIC).
[b]Imports/Delivery − exports and imports.
Source: L. A. Davies, "New Definition of 'High Tech' Reveals that U.S. Competitiveness in This Area Has Been Declining," Business America, 18 October 1982.

linked to future economic priorities. As long as these priorities remain undefined, Washington will be incapable of articulating a broad and consistent economic policy. Rather, predominantly caustic and reactive decisions may be expected, with a high degree of influence from pressure groups and, on occasion, conflicting interests.

Japan has become a favorite target for U.S. rhetoric and actions. First, Japan maintains a significant trade surplus with the United States, both in overall trade and in manufactured items specifically. In the first three quarters of 1982, this surplus reached an annual rate of $18 billion. Secondly, although Japan is a member of GATT and maintains a low level of custom duties, most U.S. analysts see Japan as a paradise of nontariff protectionism. The United States' official view is that Japan, the second largest capitalist market in the world, does not participate equitably in the maintenance of an open trade system. In the words of one State Department official, although Japan adheres to official regulations, "It still maintains a set of internal regulations which inhibit imports."[10] On the other hand, other studies highlight different aspects that often pass unnoticed in official U.S. analyses. The high positive balance in the trade of Japanese manufactured goods and in their bilateral relations with the United States is offset by an extremely negative balance in the trade of primary products (on which they are greatly dependent) and in trade with other parts of the world, particularly Asia. Over the last five years, Japan has recorded both positive and negative balances in its trade and current account balance.

In fact, this foreign trade structure favors the expansion of sectors—such as manufacturing—with greater potential for technical innovation and increase in productivity. This lays the basis for the development of a "virtuous circle": growth in production—growth in productivity—growth in market. This situation makes the application of structural adjustments linked to the deterioration of certain sectors and to the development of new activities more feasible and less traumatic. During periods of general expansion, this dynamism is not necessarily in conflict with the overall situation. However, in conditions of stagnation and recession it becomes extremely irritating for those countries unable to attain the "virtuous circle." This discrepancy is at the core of current trade conflicts, both with Japan and with other developed and developing countries.

The European Economic Community has also been facing U.S. pressure mainly, although not exclusively, with respect to the agricultural sector. U.S.-European conflicts on matters of trade are long-standing; in the contemporary period, they date back to the creation of the EEC. Indeed, one of the main reasons for U.S. insistence on the 1967 international tariff reductions of the Kennedy Round was to counteract the possible effects of the EEC as a mechanism to distort and divert trade flows. In general, the European position favored discriminatory attitudes and permitted the conclusion of sectoral or bilateral agreements in terms basically defined by the national authorities. This position is in conflict with the United States' traditional insistence on nondiscrimination and multilateralism. These differences are closely related to the nature of European and North American external links, and to the role played by the domestic economy in each nation-state. It is for this reason that these issues are difficult to negotiate.

Finally, the newly industrialized countries have also been affected by U.S. pressure. These countries' economies enjoy competitive advantages in a number of industrial products, and their influence on the economies of advanced capitalist countries has increased correspondingly. Normally, the sectors most affected by NIC influence are those sectors within developed economies that are most severely affected by structural adjustments. This has resulted in pressure to increase protectionism or eliminate access by NICs to the benefit of the system of preferences. These conflicts are particularly pronounced because NIC exports are normally concentrated in a limited range of products. This increases the vulnerability of these countries to U.S. decisions. Although some studies have shown that imports from NICs are not a significant cause of the fall in production of manufactured goods, the increase in unemployment, or the closure of businesses, these countries in particular have suffered from U.S. protectionism.

Protectionism in Congress

Protectionism in Congress toward industrialized countries inspired the introduction of legislative proposals (opposed by the Reagan administration) aimed at securing equal reciprocal treatment[11] and assuring local inputs into production.

The most important legislative proposal concerning reciprocity was the Reciprocal Trade and Investment Act (S.144) introduced by Senator John Danforth (R, Mo.). This bill contains powerful mechanisms to enable the United States, in Senator Danforth's words, "to seek nothing more or nothing less than the opportunity to compete on an equal footing." In order to improve the U.S. trade stance, the bill reinforces presidential authority to counteract unfair trade practices. The bill proposes, among other things; (1) that the U.S. trade representative expose and condemn unfair trade practices rather than having to wait for the affected party to take proceedings; (2) that the government be authorized to withdraw concessions or impose surcharges or other restrictions against countries that continue to maintain barriers against U.S. suppliers; (3) that the president's negotiating authority be expanded, particularly in relation to trade in services and high technology products; (4) that the administration be required to submit an annual report to Congress, through the trade representative, not only on existing barriers to U.S. exports of goods (including agricultural products) and services, but also on measures being taken by the administration to have these barriers removed. Senator Danforth's proposal also expanded the definition of international trade to specifically include agricultural products, services, intellectual property, high technology exports, and investment abroad (especially if this involves trade in goods and services).

Although the administration does not fully support Senator Danforth's bill, it might eventually do so to prevent further protectionist legislation. Indeed, S.144 commands considerable support from organizations such as the National Association of Manufacturers, the Business Roundtable, the Chamber of Commerce, the National Foreign Trade Council, and the American Farm Bureau.

The most important draft bill on local inputs, presented by Representative Richard Ottinger (D, N.Y.), is the fair practices in automotive parts bill, H.R.1234, which has received firm support from the United Auto Workers and the AFL-CIO. The Reagan administration has repeatedly made it clear that it will veto any legislation of this type approved by Congress.

In relations with the NICs, the "graduation principle" has become an important instrument at the disposal of the U.S. government. According to this principle, those countries that have already attained a certain level of industrialization should cease to enjoy preferences granted to relatively less developed countries. Discussions on the mechanisms of graduation will likely be very intense in the near future concerning the Generalized System of Preferences (GSP), which expires on 1 January 1985. The central question is how graduation should be determined and which countries should be the major beneficiaries of the program. Possible alternatives include the total exclusion of certain countries from the list of beneficiaries; the exclusion of developing countries whose annual exports to the United States exceed $250 million; a reduction from 50 percent to 35–40 percent for the competitive need clause; and the exclusion of countries unwilling to eliminate export requirements for U.S. investors and other "unfair" trade practices.

Protectionism by Sector

During the tenure of the present Republican administration, particularly intense trade conflicts have arisen in the textile, automobile, and steel industries. In December 1981, a new version of the Multifiber Agreement was concluded. This agreement regulates the import of textiles and garments into industrialized markets. In accordance with the new agreement—the most restrictive to date— the United States and other industrialized countries will be able to establish import growth levels below the 6 percent per annum scheduled for each individual country. This decision affects the major Southeast Asian and Latin American exporters.

Automotive production continues to experience sharp contractions in the United States. In view of the growing popularity of Japanese cars, official and unofficial negotiations with Japan led to the establishment, in May 1981, of a "voluntary agreement to restrict exports." According to this agreement, sales will be maintained at 92 percent of the 1980 level during the first year of operation; in the second year, sales may increase by 16 percent of the total market increase.

In the context of tensions that threatened to trigger a large-scale confrontation between the EEC and the United States, in October 1982 European countries agreed to limit their exports of certain types of steel to the United States. A number of U.S. firms had applied to the International Trade Commission to have countervailing duties applied to imports from some European countries, based on the argument that these imports were being subsidized.

In short, U.S. trade policy has been guided by a set of formal and comprehensive principles complemented by periods of national pressure and sectoral negotiation where necessary. The introduction of legislation on the regulation of reciprocity and local input requirements for production reflects increasing pressure for a more aggressive U.S. trade policy. The persistence of slow growth conditions or economic stagnation will aggravate these demands. Certainly, attention should be paid to the repeated proposals on adopting an industrial policy in the United States to stimulate more organized development in certain sectors and effect structural adjustments in others. This would naturally have consequences for international trade.

Financial Policy

Since 1981, U.S. domestic economic policy has had significant repercussions on the world economy, particularly with regard to financing. The monetary policy pursued by the Federal Reserve has affected both capital movements and the exchange rate of the dollar. In this section, some aspects of U.S. financial policy will be discussed with reference to multilateral organizations and bilateral aid programs. The more general, but nonetheless important, questions of the international impact of domestic policies will be discussed in the following section.

U.S. financial and aid policies revolve around two fundamental axes: on the one hand, encouragement and support of private capital flows through the use of public funds; on the other, a preference for bilateral rather than multilateral mechanisms in the use of public funds. We have already identified some measures applied by the Reagan administation to stimulate private capital flows to developing countries. As far as bilateral versus multilateral aid is concerned, the Republican administration prefers the former as more effective in the promotion and guarantee of U.S. strategic interests and security. It is easier to exercise control over the destination and use of bilateral aid, as well as to establish more immediate and direct links between available resources and needs. Due to these considerations, the Reagan administration is attempting to reverse the recent trend in the U.S. budget towards an increase in multilateral aid over bilateral aid, through reducing U.S. commitments in "soft" lines of credit to multilateral development banks and by progressively cutting back paid-up capital increases.

With regard to bilateral aid, a notable change in priorities has occurred. The Reagan administration came to office harboring serious doubts as to the value of development aid, particularly in terms of the new guidelines adopted in 1973, which emphasized the alleviation of poverty and the basic needs of the masses. Budget allocations for development aid have remained more or less constant, a contraction in real terms (see Table 19). However, this restriction did not extend to budget items related to the promotion of U.S. security interests. This is illustrated by the Economic Support Fund (administered by AID), which provides balance-of-payments assistance to countries considered to be of strategic importance to the United States. The emphasis on security is further reinforced by the handling of the military assistance budget (Table 19).

Indeed, these changes occur within the context of a more permanent trend towards a reduction in U.S. foreign aid. Excluding military assistance, when all aid programs are computed (multilateral

Table 19. U.S. Military and Economic Assistance to Developing Countries, 1981–1984 (thousands US$)

Form of Aid	Fiscal Year			
	1981	1982	1983[a]	1984[b]
Development aid	1.7	1.9	1.9	1.9
PL 480 food aid	1.6	1.4	1.5	1.5
Economic Support Fund	2.2	2.8	3.1	3.0
Loans guaranteed for the sale of military equipment abroad	2.5	3.1	4.2	4.4
Military assistance grants	0.2	0.2	0.5	0.8

[a]Includes the proposed settlement.
[b]Proposed.

Source: U.S. Agency for International Development, Congressional Presentation FY 1984 (Washington, D.C.: AID, 1984).

assistance, bilateral development aid, PL 480 food aid, and non-military bilateral aid for security), systematic contractions both in real terms and in relation to the GNP or federal expenditure may be observed (see Table 20).

Military aid is channeled through institutions such as the International Monetary Fund, the World Bank, and regional development banks. The U.S. position with regard to each is outlined below.

International Monetary Fund

Traditionally, the U.S. government has been a strong defender and advocate of the IMF. This organization has normally been viewed by the United States as a fundamental agent in the system of international monetary and financial stability, and as a mechanism for assisting countries experiencing balance-of-payments difficulties. The IMF and the Reagan administration are both clearly in favor of market mechanisms and private enterprise. Furthermore, the IMF's programs and policies reveal a clearly anti-inflationary approach.

However, some important officials in the present Republican administration—particularly the under-secretary for monetary af-

Table 20. Federal Expenditure for Overseas Economic and Financial Aid, Fiscal Years 1961-1983 (billions US$)[a]

Period or Fiscal Year[b]	Expenditure Current Prices	Constant Dollars[c]	% of Total Federal Expenditure	% of GNP
1961-65	6.6	10.5	3.25	0.56
1966-70	3.9	9.9	2.34	0.38
1971-75	3.0	5.5	1.16	0.27
1976-78	4.0	5.3	0.97	0.26
1979	4.7	5.4	0.96	0.20
1980	5.6	5.6	0.97	0.21
1981	6.3	5.7	0.96	0.22
1982[d]	6.0	5.4	0.91	na[e]
1983[f]	7.0	na	0.92	na

[a]Figured according to the OECD definition of official development aid.
[b]Figures for 1961-1978 are annual averages.
[c]For 1967-1977 the OECD deflator was used for U.S. official development aid. U.S. wholesale price indices were used for the remainder.
[d]Estimated.
[e]na = not available.
[f]Proposed.

Source: R. Newfarmer, "US Foreign Economic Policy Toward Latin America" (1982, mimeo.).

fairs, Beryl Sprinkel—have from the outset been skeptical about the IMF. IMF loans were sometimes seen as aid programs that allowed countries in difficulty to adopt wasteful policies and postpone adjustments. These officials were particularly opposed to certain recent trends in standby agreements, which they viewed as giving too much flexibility to the regulations. Two such reforms were the adoption of the expanded facility and the 1979 guidelines for the IMF technical team, requiring social and political objectives of member countries to be taken into account.

On taking office, the general goals of the Reagan administration for the IMF and its policies were (1) to reduce the lending role of the fund, by encouraging the use of credit from international commercial banks; (2) to make conditionality more rigid; and (3) to encourage the adoption of policies consistent with its own deflationist approach. These three principles coincided with the general outlook of the new U.S. administration. The IMF should strictly confine itself to its task of last resort lender, imposing strict adjustment conditions and guaranteeing their fulfillment. The displacement of multilateral financial agencies by private banks in maintaining international capital flows was seen as a positive factor that demonstrated the "magic of the market."

The first significant shift in the attitude of the Reagan administration occurred at the IMF's annual meeting held in September 1982 in Toronto, when the problem of the foreign debt of the developing countries was raised in all its magnitude. The United States' position regarding the fund's role was divided between treasury officials—ideologically less flexible—and the Federal Reserve. The prevailing position before the meeting was generally in support of an increase of between 20 and 25 percent of IMF quotas. U.S. officials feared that a greater increase would detract from the rigor of conditionality and reinforce the trend towards greater flexibility in the role of the IMF, making it just one more development aid agency. The administration also feared excessive increases in international liquidity and the possible inflationary implications.

The accumulation of tensions on the international financial scene during the second half of 1982 was a decisive factor in shaping the flexible position adopted by the United States. In February 1983, the administration finally accepted a 47.5 percent increase in quotas, effective as of the beginning of 1984. The United States also agreed to strengthen and reinforce the General Loan Agreement by increasing its resources from $7 to $20 billion and authorizing its utilization by developing countries. This measure was interpreted as an attempt by the United States to maintain tighter control over the increased resources, to the extent that industrialized countries participating in the General Loan Agreement maintain control over the use of those resources.

The world financial crisis of the second half of 1982 also led to a significant change in the relations between commercial banks and the IMF. As a result of the sharp contraction in loans from private banks to developing countries in 1982, the IMF decided to subject their own credit packages to the maintenance of credit flows by private banks to economies in difficulty. The Reagan administration indicated its support of such actions, although the principles it professes are contrary to this policy. In fact, the Federal Reserve in New York—entrusted with the international activities of the reserve system—served as a meeting place between the IMF and private banks for discussions on particular national cases.

Several high-ranking officials, including Secretary of the Treasury Donald Regan and Secretary of State George Schultz, publicly requested that banks continue to extend new credits to developing countries. The Federal Reserve Board extended short-term lines of credit to a number of countries in crisis. This level of international action is certainly not in keeping with the original definitions of principle advanced by the Reagan administration. It was a response to pressures imposed by the crisis on the international scene.

Towards the end of 1982, the Senior Interagency Group on International Economic Policy (SIG-IEP) approved a five-point plan to deal with the delicate international financial situation. The points confirm the basis of the administration's policies.

1. IMF resources should be increased, with a view to helping developing countries to meet their debt servicing requirements while maintaining essential imports.
2. The IMF and the U.S. government should continue to encourage commercial banks to refinance loans that fall due, and extend new lines to countries that adopt programs in conjunction with the fund.
3. While programs are being negotiated with the IMF, short-term bilateral lines of credit should be extended in the form of "bridging loans."
4. As the economies of the United States and other industrialized countries experience a gradual recovery, they will provide a healthier international economic environment.
5. Finally, developing countries should adjust their economies—with the advice of the IMF—by restricting demand and liberalizing their trade and exchange policy.

Both the Treasury Department and the State Department recognized that this five-point strategy was essentially sound, and that the main dangers to the international financial system were being contained.

Gradually, then, the set of principles initially proposed by the administration regarding the IMF were progressively modified by force of circumstance. Such pragmatic actions, however, did not qualitatively alter the approach of the Reagan administration toward critical international financial problems.

Multilateral Development Banks

From the outset, the prevailing view in the Republican administration was that the assistance provided by multilateral development banks (MDBs) should be trimmed together with the dismantling of the "welfare state" at the national level. It was also felt that because the United States had been losing its influence on these organizations, they were no longer adequately serving U.S. interests.

In February 1982, the Treasury Department published an exhaustive report prepared the year before, entitled *United States Participation in Multilateral Development Banks in the 1980s*. This report attempts to assess the degree of similarity between U.S. objectives and the activity of MDBs, and recommends some future policy guidelines for U.S. participation in such organizations. The conclusions of this report did not support the notion that the MDBs were acting as charity organizations that did not adequately reflect the strategic interests of the United States. On the contrary, the treasury's report concluded that the MDBs are contributing to the overall economic objectives by encouraging developing countries to participate fully in a freer international trade and capital movements system. It stated that U.S. commercial objectives are being facilitated by the creation of greater opportunities for trade, investment, and finance for the United States, and that political and strategic objectives are encouraged by the climate of greater stability promoted by MDB contributions to economic growth. Nevertheless, the document also pointed out that despite the usefulness of the MDBs' activity, the budgetary goals of the government required some reductions in the United States' contribution. In effect, the administration's domestic policy meant a reduction of U.S. budgetary support in the allocation of resources to the MDBs.

The World Bank. The Reagan administration's substantive proposals concerning the World Bank were no novelty. Such proposals have been part of official policy for most of the life of this institution. At issue was rather the form and rate of their application, and the extent to which timely implementation of such policies would be an effective substitute for a greater volume of resources.

To begin with, the administration requested a significant reduction in real terms in the United States' contribution to the soft credit lines, particularly those of the International Development Association (IDA), which channels resources to the poorest countries. According to the administration, the World Bank could make better use of its resources if it applied the principles of graduation more strictly and subjected them to certain policy reforms. The MDBs could also help developing countries to establish domestic capital markets and obtain credits on the private international financial market, through cofinancing and through expanding the activities of the International Finance Corporation (IFC).

The World Bank has a long-standing policy of restricting access of beneficiary countries to concessional credit as their level of development rises. Countries "graduate" from full access to soft credit and then to a combination of soft credit with credit at market rates. Eventually, countries no longer have access to the concessional credit window. The U.S. approach of applying stricter graduation criteria coincided with the progressive inability of developing countries to obtain commercial credit in the private international financial system.

In general, the administration has actively supported the International Finance Corporation and cofinancing practices. However, in this case again, the economic conditions prevailing at the beginning of the eighties limited the growth of these programs. During fiscal year 1982, IFC investments fell below the 1980 level. In this same period, the number of cofinancing projects decreased by approximately 25 percent. The structural adjustment loans program instituted by the World Bank in 1979 could provide this institution with the capacity to influence the macroeconomic and sectoral policies of beneficiary countries, in keeping with the preferences of the Reagan administration.

The U.S. government's emphasis on the graduation policy and its encouragement of private capital flows and efficient economic management reaffirmed old ideas accepted and implemented by the World Bank. However, the application of such policies—with different levels of flexibility—is clearly no substitute for the transfer of resources that the MDBs hypothetically promote.

In this context, the Reagan administration has constantly insisted on the need to limit the expansion of World Bank credits. It decided to meet the commitments assumed by the Carter administration to the International Development Association's sixth capital replenishment, but at a much slower rate than the three years originally envisaged. The United States' failure to meet their commitments in the designated time period has reduced the association's loan capacity by 35 to 40 percent, thus achieving the U.S. objective of reducing the supply of soft credits and applying a stricter graduation policy to reserve resources for the poorest countries. Although negotiations have commenced for the seventh replenishment, a serious negotiating attitude is not expected from the United States until the sixth replenishment has been substantially completed. The former president of the World Bank, Robert McNamara, declared that the IDA was "bankrupt" due to its inability to meet its obligations. In fact, 1984 and 1985 will be extremely difficult years with the low availability of resources in this organization.

The Inter-American Development Bank (IDB). The outcome of negotiations for the last replenishment of IDB resources reflected the effect of U.S. policy on the MDBs. The Reagan administration led the action of the multilateral organizations in the direction it desired, although it had to compromise on the speed and extent of the reform.

In the specific case of the IDB, despite the fact that (hard) regular lines of credit will continue to grow in real terms between 1983 and 1986 (from $1.86 billion in 1982 to $3.45 billion in 1986), the Special Operations Fund's (soft) loans will decrease in nominal terms (from $625 million in 1982 to an average of $500 million between 1983 and 1986). The U.S. position has alerted analysts to the likelihood of this last program being completely discontinued in the next capital replenishment. The graduation principle was also maintained, although not at the rate of application originally preferred by the administration. On the basis of the United States position, the percentage of paid-up capital was also reduced from 6.4 percent to 4.5 percent.

The Reagan administration attempted to encourage two other objectives in its IDB policy. It recommended the establishment of an inter-American investment corporation to promote private capital investment in Latin America and the Caribbean, particularly in small and medium-sized enterprises. It also tried to use IDB activities to promote its own foreign policy objectives in Central America, but these efforts met with only partial success.

**The Effects of U.S. Economic Policy
on the World Economy**

International economic policy was a low priority for the Republican government due to the Reagan administration's orientation and thinking on both overall foreign policy and domestic economic policy. As President Reagan himself pointed out to the 1982 joint meeting of the IMF and the World Bank, "the most important contribution that a country can make to world development is the application of sound domestic economic policies." Consequently, the ERP was assigned top priority and would receive the most attention and emphasis.

The promotion of domestic economic growth together with price stability would have a positive influence on the international economy, laying the basis for collective expansion. The stability of the U.S. economy would be of great significance to the rest of the world, for the United States is the main market, and its currency still constitutes the axis of the international monetary system. A strong and stable dollar would create a general climate of noninflationary expansion.

Obviously, the effects of the ERP on the U.S. economy would be felt abroad, a reminder of the international significance of U.S. economic development. The market mechanisms would serve as transmission channels through two basic mechanisms: real channels and financial-monetary channels.

Real Channels

Trade flows constitute the main real channel through which recessive effects are transmitted on an international scale. The slow growth or contraction of the U.S. market reduces the growth of the rest of the world's exports, and through the multiplying effect of the external sector, reduces overall economic activity. This creates a vicious circle with a strong tendency towards cumulative contraction. During 1982 there was a significant contraction in U.S. imports covering a vast range of products and regions of origin (Table 21). The most significant drop by product type was registered in oil imports, and by origin in imports from OPEC. During 1981 and

Table 21. Growth in U.S. Imports (annual %)

	1975-79	1980	1981	1982[a]
Total imports	21.2	17.8	5.8	-5.4
Oil imports	22.3	31.3	-2.3	-21.6
Nonoil imports	20.8	12.4	9.6	1.4
Imports from industrialized countries	19.1	13.4	12.3	1.6
Imports from OPEC countries	24.3	23.4	-10.2	-35.0
Imports from other countries	22.8	24.3	9.0	2.0

[a]Annual rate for first three quarters of 1982.
[b]This includes Latin American republics, other countries of the Western Hemisphere, and other non-OPEC Asian and African countries.

Source: Office of the President, *Economic Report of the President,* 1983 (Washington, D.C.: GPO, 1983).

1982 the United States shifted its basic sources of supply from OPEC member countries to other, nonmember oil exporters, notably Mexico.

U.S. imports were partially stimulated by the revaluation of the dollar, which served to make foreign products more competitive. Yet with the sharp contraction in domestic demand, particularly in key sectors such as the iron, steel, and automotive industries, the presence of imported products became a significant source of tensions, conflicts, and pressure for a higher level of protectionism.

The contraction of the U.S. market and the contraction in the market of the industrialized countries generally considerably affected countries exporting primary products. These countries were doubly affected by a reduction in volume and a drop in prices. During 1981 and 1982 the prices of the most important primary products dropped considerably in the international market, affecting the export earnings of the economies that depend on them. This in turn reduced their import capacity, creating successive cycles of contraction in international trade. The prices of a wide range of

Table 22. Primary Product Prices in the International Market (1975 index = 100)

	1979	1980	1981 I	II	III	IV	1982 I	II
Primary products	150	174	163	157	143	142	141	135
Food	148	171	159	147	133	134	134	124
Agricultural raw mat.	188	210	203	187	175	164	162	160
Nonferrous minerals and metals	125	149	142	143	147	148	149	137

Source: International Trade, 1981–1982 (Geneva: GATT, 1982).

primary products were depressed, and this contraction in prices spread to raw materials, which, like oil, had managed to maintain high prices for the better part of the seventies (see Table 22). When these countries became highly indebted, the financial restriction of 1982 caused an acute crisis in the balance of payments, threatening the entire international financial system with collapse.

Financial-Monetary Channels

During the early eighties, financial-monetary channels played an absolute central role in transmitting downward trends from the United States to the rest of the world economy. There is a close link between the national financial and monetary markets and between these and the "supranational" Euro-currency market, particularly in the advanced capitalist countries. As a result, relative returns (including exchange risks) on the different types of assets are a central determinant of short-term capital flows. These flows are, in turn, an important determinant of the fluctuations in exchange rates.

As already mentioned, Reagan's economic policy and the "disinflation" process in the United States caused a considerable increase in real interest rates. This increase critically affected the rest of the international economy. The growth in relative returns on assets quoted in dollars increased their demand, which at the initial stage is tantamount to an increase in the dollar demand. This resulted in a growing differential between short-term interest rates in the United States and in other industrialized countries, a decisive factor that strengthened the dollar in relation to other currencies. Furthermore, to the extent that the Federal Reserve pursued a monetary policy of nonintervention in exchange markets, these trends became much more pronounced.

It is appropriate to make some relevant points about the dynamics of the industrialized bloc. In the first place, despite the increasingly important role of the German mark, the establishment of the European Monetary System, and other measures, this region continues to have a sensitive monetary dependence on the United States. Since the Second World War, Europe has fluctuated between a shortage and an abundance of dollars, between an expensive and a cheap dollar. These fluctuations generally coincide with the successive contraction and expansion phases in the United States, in relation to European economies. This long-term link has become more irritating with the application in the United States of monetary policies to control the money stock, and with the resulting fluctuations in interest rates. There is a close relationship between these fluctuations and those of the European monetary markets, which have been particularly acute since 1979.

The European countries had three possible responses to the increase in short-term interest rates in the United States. The first was to accept the depreciation of their currencies in relation to the dollar, or limit said depreciation by intervention in the exchange markets. The latter alternative has clear limitations in terms of the availablity of foreign exchange on the part of central banks. The second possibility was to increase returns on assets quoted in their own currency through monetary restriction to reduce the existing differential in favor of U.S. rates. This action would have recessive effects. The third alternative was to take more long-term measures aimed at controlling the exchange market and speculative capital outflows—which would isolate the national financial-monetary market from the international one—or to initiate long-term actions toward the convergence of domestic economic development with that of the United States.

During the first part of the eighties, the European countries reacted with a combination of the first two alternatives. The results were first, increased instability in exchange rates; second, an interruption in the relation between the cycle and the interest rate levels; third, an increase in interest rates and subsequent recessive trends; and fourth, dependence of European recovery on conditions prevailing in the U.S. economy and on the economic policy of the United States.

The recessive trends in the U.S. economy had a direct effect on developing countries by increasing the cost of servicing debts. To the extent that a developing country's foreign debt—particularly the debt contracted with private financial sources—was negotiated with fluctuating interest rates, the increases in the interest rate automatically multiplied the debt-service burden. This trend reflected the close relationship between the interest rates on the U.S. financial market and the prevailing rates on the private international market. Developing countries were also affected, although in a different way, by the same mechanisms that influenced the European economies. The opening up of the financial markets in several countries and their integration into international markets during the second half of the seventies created an important channel of influence on domestic economic policy.

In short, the economies of the rest of the world—in both industrialized and developing countries—suffered the consequences of the impact of the ERP on the U.S. economy. The contraction of trade flows initiated a vicious circle of successive reductions. In the developing countries, this caused a contraction of markets and a drop in the prices of their primary export products. The conditions of productive stagnation and high unemployment in the United States also intensified protectionist pressures, further aggravating the depressive effects on the entire international economy. Financial-monetary channels spread recessive trends to those countries whose markets are integrated into the international system, and also to developing economies through the cost of financing and of servicing debts. Table 23 shows the generalized compression of the expansion rate.

The recessive picture was complicated by the decision of U.S. authorities to refrain from intervening in the exchange markets except in the case of extreme instability. This was an immediate corollary of the Federal Reserve's decision to control monetary aggregates. Intervention to sustain or affect the parity of the dollar inevitably affects the domestic money supply and can eventually

Table 23. World Growth in Real GNP, 1978–1982

	1978	1979	1980	1981	1982
World Growth	3.8	2.8	1.8	1.8	−0.2
Developed Countries	4.1	3.5	1.2	1.4	−0.5
United States	4.8	3.2	−0.2	2.0	−1.8
Japan	5.1	5.6	4.2	2.0	2.5
Canada	3.7	3.0	—	3.0	−5.0
EEC	3.1	3.4	1.3	−0.4	0.3
Others	2.1	−1.7	4.0	5.2	na[a]
Developing countries	4.3	4.1	4.5	2.7	0.8
Oil exporters	6.7	3.2	2.0	−0.5	1.2
Others	3.3	4.5	5.6	3.1	0.7
Socialist countries	4.2	1.6	1.9	1.2	1.4

[a]na = not available.

Source: Office of the President, Economic Report of the President, 1983 (Washington, D.C.: GPO, 1983).

counteract the objectives of the Federal Reserve. U.S. authorities had maintained a policy of sporadic intervention since the generalized institution of flexible exchange rates in 1973. In November of that year, and at the inception of the new administration in 1981, the United States intervened extensively in the exchange markets. The new government decided, however, that such intervention was ineffective and even self-defeating and decided to suspend all action except in situations of extreme crisis. This caused great fluctuations in exchange rates and a general revaluation of the dollar.

Notes

1. Alexander Haig, Statement before the Senate Committee on Foreign Relations, 19 March 1981, Department of State Bulletin, April 1981.

2. Myer Rashish, "The International Economic Policy of the U.S. and Its Impact on the Development Countries" (Address delivered to the Korean-American Association, Seoul, 22 June 1981).

3. Ronald Reagan, Message to the Joint Annual Assembly of the International Monetary Fund and the World Bank, Washington, D.C., 29 September 1981 (telex).

4. Ibid.

5. In fact, the transfer of these trends became a new "dollar diplomacy." See R. Bouzas, "The Economic Policy of the Republican Administration. (Bases for Future Disorder)" in H. Jaguaribe, *América Latina en la política international de los años ochenta* (Buenos Aires: Editorial de Belgrado, 1982).

6. R. L. Barovick, "Bilateral Investment Treaties," *Business America*, 23 August 1983, pp. 3–5.

7. Ibid.

8. Statement made by U.S. Trade Representative William Brock at the signing of a BIT between the United States and Egypt. Ibid.

9. Other measures by the administration have also heightened this conflict. The decision to reduce the funds destined to subsidize unemployed workers, made as a consequence of competition from imports (trade adjustment assistance), undoubtedly affected the intensity of protectionist pressures within the United States. According to the administration's prevailing criteria, measures such as these were extremely ineffective and delayed the structural adjustment, which could be made with fewer impediments through the free operation of market mechanisms.

10. John H. Holdridge, "Japan and the US: A Cooperative Relationship," Declaration to the Committee on Foreign Affairs by the Assistant Secretary for Pacific and East Asian Affairs, *Department of State Bulletin*, April 1982.

11. For a discussion on reciprocity legislation in trade, see W. Cline, "Reciprocity: A New Approach to World Trade Policy?" *Economic Policy Analysis* (Institute for International Economies) 2 (September 1982).

3

Economic Relations Between Latin America and the United States in the Early Eighties

The Recent Context of Latin American–U.S. Economic Relations

Economic relations between the United States and Latin America changed significantly over the last two decades. Latin America diversified its foreign economic relations at the same time as it began coordinating its efforts in international economic policy through multilateral channels. Latin America has not submitted a joint proposal to the United States since the 1969 CECLA (Special Commission for Latin American Coordination) conference at Viña del Mar and the subsequent meeting of Latin American representatives with President Nixon. In December 1981, Latin America adopted, within the framework of SELA, the Declaration of Panama on Economic Relations with the United States of America, but has yet to submit it to the United States for approval. The delay is due to important changes both in inter-American and international relations. Latin America became increasingly important at the international level; the larger countries of the region began to formulate more-global political and economic strategies; the private sectors have increasingly replaced government agencies in economic

Table 24. The U.S. and Latin American Share of Reciprocal Trade (% of total trade)

| | United States | | Latin America | |
Year	Exports to Latin America	Imports from Latin America	Exports to the United States	Imports from the United States
1950	27.9	35.1	48.3	50.1
1961	18.5	24.5	36.7	38.0
1965	15.4	19.0	33.0	36.6
1970	15.2	14.1	33.2	34.9
1973	14.3	14.7	34.4	30.1
1975	16.1	18.0	35.3	28.8
1978	15.5	12.1	34.1	28.7
1979	15.8	14.2	35.3	29.8
1980	17.6	15.7	34.0	30.4

Sources: For 1950–1970: UN, *United Nations Yearbook of International Trade Statistics* and *United Nations Monthly Bulletin of Statistics,* various years; SELA, *Ley de comercio internacional de Estados Unidos de America,* June 1979, Table II-2. For 1970–1979: University of Cambridge, *World Trade and Finance: Prospects for the 1980's* (Cambridge, Eng., December 1980), App. B. For 1980: U.S. Department of Commerce, *Highlights of U.S. Exports and Import Trade* (Washington, D.C.: GPO, 1981); and *UNCTAD Handbook of International Trade and Development,* Supplement 1981 (New York: United Nations, 1982).

relations; European and Japanese economic presence increased in the region; and the international system itself evolved toward a more clearly multipolar political and economic situation.

A clear trend toward a relative decrease in U.S. involvement in Latin American economic relations emerged in the sixties. The data in Table 24 indicate a progressive decline in mutual trade with the United States as a percentage of the region's total trade. This trend stabilized in the seventies due to the oil trade.

Changes on the financial scene have been even more drastic, owing, for example, to the increasing substitution of official credit sources by private ones and the replacement of direct investment by financial transfers. Table 25 shows the sharp drop in U.S. official credit as a percentage of the total external financing of the region. Direct U.S. investment also dropped as a percentage of Latin

Table 25. Capital Flows to Latin America (millions US$)

	1961	1965	1970	1975	1980
Net bilateral flows from the United States	732.5	498.7	685.5	635.7	653.0
Total net flows of external financing to Latin America	1,834.2	1,571.1	3,794.9	12,227.0	22,100.0
U.S. flows as percentage of total	39.9%	31.7%	18.1%	5.2%	3.0%

Source: Inter-American Development Bank, *External Financing of the Latin American Countries* (Washington, D.C., December 1981), Table 4.

America's total gross external financing. According to the Inter-American Development Bank, U.S. foreign investment, which represented 20 percent of gross external financing for 1971–1975, dropped to 10 percent for 1975–1979. U.S. foreign investment did retain its share of total direct foreign investment in the region.

Trade Balance

In more global terms, Latin America increased in relative economic importance to the United States. In terms of population, gross national product, and per capita product, Latin America's position improved vis-à-vis the United States (see Table 26). The region also maintained growth rates higher than those of the U.S. economy. In the manufacturing sector Latin America's share in world production of manufactured goods rose from 4.6 percent in 1964 to 5.7 percent in 1977; the U.S. share decreased from 29.4 percent to 22.4 percent for the same period (see Table 27).

These changes undoubtedly reflect the economic potential of the region as well as the relative stagnation of the U.S. economy in the postwar period. The economic vibrance of Europe, Japan, and the developing countries provided an opportunity for Latin America to diversify its external economic links. In spite of these developments, a basic imbalance in economic relations between the United States and Latin America persists due to the differences in relative development levels and the mechanisms and principles that govern international economic relations.

First of all, Latin America's current account deficit with the United States has continued to increase, from US $1,466 million in 1970 to US $14,451 million in 1980 (see Table 28). This increase was basically due to the performance of the services account. Although there was in general a positive balance in merchandise trade, this was due to the oil trade. The U.S. surplus in the trade of manufactures with Latin America rose from US $4 billion in 1970 to US $17.3 billion in 1980. This increase meant that the surplus in U.S. trade of manufactures with the region moved from 127 percent of the total U.S. surplus in that sector for 1970 to 313 percent ten years later.

In 1981, four Latin American countries (Mexico, Argentina, Colombia, and Chile) were among the fifteen largest trading partners of the U.S. with which the U.S. maintained a surplus trade position (a total of US $6.9 billion in favor of the United States). In contrast, of the fifteen largest U.S. trading partners with whom the greatest deficits were registered, there were only three Latin American and Caribbean countries (Netherlands Antilles, Trinidad, Bahamas) with a total of US $4.4 billion.

Second, the traditional trend in Latin America's declining terms of trade has continued, with the exception of oil. For non-oil exporting countries, this ratio fell from 100 in 1970 to 76 in 1980 (see Table 29). This unfavorable trend in relative nonoil prices, combined with marked income instability, has become a serious obstacle to the region's stable development.

Third, the intensification of U.S. protectionist policies, especially in the late seventies and early eighties, has limited market access for the region's products, particularly for manufactures. The U.S. Generalized System of Preferences applies to a small number of products and is subject to numerous unilateral and discriminatory restrictions. The United States maintains a level of effective protection that discriminates against the region's manufactured products.

Table 26. Relative Economic Size of Latin America and the United States

	Population (millions)			GNP (billions current US$)			GNP per capita (current US$)		
	1960	1970	1980	1960	1970	1980	1960	1970	1980
U.S.(1)	180.7	203.8	227.6	509.0	989.0	2,377.0	2,817	4,851	10,775
L.A.(2)	207.1	312.7	360.7	66.5	158.2	617.0	321	577	1,714
(1)÷(2)	0.87	0.65	0.63	7.7	6.3	3.9	8.8	8.4	6.3

Source: For 1960, United Nations, World Statistics in Brief, 1st ed. (New York: UN, 1976). For 1970 and 1980, United Nations, World Statistics in Brief, 6th ed. (New York: UN, 1981).

Table 27. The U.S. and Latin American Share in World Output of Manufactured Goods (%)

	1964	1973	1977
United States	29.4	23.9	22.4
Latin America	4.6	5.3	5.7

Source: University of Cambridge, Department of Applied Economics, World Trade and Finance: Prospects for the 1980's (Cambridge, Eng., December 1980), Tables 1.14 and 1.12.

Table 28. Latin America's Current Account with the United States, 1970–1980 (millions US$)

	1970	1975	1980
Exports of goods and services	8,407	21,384	52,922
Imports of goods and services	10,395	25,448	68,553
Current account balance	−1,466	−3,412	−14,451

Source: U.S. Department of Commerce, "U.S.A. International Transactions," Survey of Current Business (Washington, D.C.), various issues.

Table 29. Latin America's Terms of Trade (1970 index = 100)

	1970	1975	1980
Latin America	100	114	123
Oil exporting countries	100	181	243
Non–oil exporting countries	100	86	76

Source: UN, Economic Commission for Latin America, *Latin America's External Economic Relations,* p. 51, Table 11.

Fourth, because the trade in manufactures between the United States and Latin America is transacted largely through transnational corporations and the channels and mechanisms of those enterprises, the control of a part of this important link remained in the hands of these enterprises. The transnational firms that operate in Latin America have shown a high propensity to import and a low propensity to export. Around 1966, about 10 percent of industrial sales by multinational subsidiaries in Latin America was composed of exports. By 1976, the proportion had fallen to 6 percent. This phenomenon, together with the imports of transnationals, led Latin American countries to design an additional set of policies on "export requirements" for foreign investment, drawing harsh criticism by the U.S. government. Moreover, the remittances from subsidiaries to headquarters in the form of profits, technical services, and royalties have grown from 12.6 percent of the total cumulative value of investment in the region in 1976 to 15.2 percent in 1979.

Financial Relations

The terms and conditions of Latin America's financial relations also deteriorated during the seventies. Increased access to the private market certainly multiplied the available resources for financing in the region. The terms of access, however, became increasingly adverse and dependent on the state of the international credit market. The growing involvement of private credit sources reduced the average amortization period from 14.3 years in 1970 to 10.7 years in 1980, and raised the cost of credit from an average interest rate of 7.1 percent in 1970 for private credit to 11.5 percent in 1980. Private sources in general applied the system of floating interest rates with resultant negative consequences when the United States began to pursue restrictive monetary policies.

Increased access to private capital markets by Latin American countries made them extremely vulnerable to the conditions prevailing on those markets. They were encouraged by the international banks to contract large amounts of credit during the high-liquidity period of 1975 to 1980. Yet when difficulties arose in some greatly indebted countries and when the state of finance markets changed as a result of U.S. economic policy, this access was almost discontinued, affecting the region's economies.

The opening of domestic financial markets and their incorporation into the international circuit provided a channel for transmitting external influences through the financial system. Domestic monetary policies became extremely susceptible to foreign influence, particularly from the United States, whose currency was used as a standard. In addition, external debt policy was subject to essentially private decisions and short-term fluctuations in the international credit market. These general trends are obviously repeated in relations with the United States.

Although Latin America increased its relative economic strength, while diversifying and elaborating its pattern of international relations, the asymmetrical and unfavorable basis of its foreign relations, particularly with the United States, has not changed substantially in the last two decades. Extremely unequal mechanisms of mutual influence still exist, and the disproportion is even increasing in some instances. Nevertheless, the changes have given Latin American countries a more solid basis on which to define more equitable and mutually beneficial relations for the parties involved.

Latin America is traditionally a priority area for the United States in crisis situations, or when the regional situation is thus considered from the point of view of U.S. security or other interests. Under the present U.S. administration, the Caribbean Basin Initiative and the attention and preferential treatment given to some highly indebted countries are proof of this. The region is faced with a difficult choice, between the privilege of and search for a "special relationship" with the United States in these times of crisis and greater autonomy. Greater autonomy would place the region in a leading position among developing economies and also allow a more constructive negotiation stance with the United States and the group of developed countries.

Trade Relations Between the United States and Latin America

The trade problems between the United States and Latin America are not new, but the critical international economic situation and its repercussions on the region have aggravated these problems. In 1982 there was a 10 percent reduction in the value of Latin America's total exports following a five-year period of rapid growth. In addition, the terms of trade declined by 7 percent, reflecting a drop in the prices of primary products that constitute the region's prime export. During the second half of 1982, the price of copper reached its lowest level in four years; sugar prices dropped to 1978 levels; and coffee prices fell sharply. This decrease even affected products that had generally maintained a relatively high price, such as oil. The decrease in world demand as a result of the international recession undoubtedly played a decisive role in price performance. The high level of real interest rates also encouraged the liquidation of stocks and discouraged the use of primary products as a refuge for speculative capital flows.

By the third quarter of 1982, Latin American exports to the United States had been reduced to an annual rate of 3 percent. The region faced both an overall increase in protectionist pressures in the United States and the contraction of the U.S. market as a result of the economic recession. There was an increase in the number of complaints from U.S. enterprises to the International Trade Administration and the International Trade Commission, asserting that certain imports from the region are subsidized and are prejudicial to U.S. industry. These complaints involved a wide range of products, from traditional exports such as beef and sugar to complex manufactured goods such as small passenger aircraft.

The general increase in U.S. protectionist pressures is associated with the long-term structural deterioration of certain industrial sectors, immediate pressures caused by the recession, and the economic policy of the present U.S. administration. The administration's emphasis on market adjustment, the reduction or suspension of aid programs to workers and companies affected by international competition, and the official rhetoric insisting on the "inequity" in

Table 30. Effective Protection Against Imports from Latin America Since the Tokyo Round (%)[a]

Import Products	United States	EEC
Primary agricultural products	10.0	15.0
Processed and other foodstuffs	20.1	69.0
Primary textile materials	14.0	22.0
Finished textile products, garments	42.5	40.0
Minerals	10.0	10.0
Light industry	18.1	13.0
Heavy industry	10.0	8.4

[a]The Tokyo Round GATT negotiations were concluded in November 1979.

Source: UN, Economic Commission for Latin America, *Latin American Foreign Economic Relations in the 80's,* p. 17, Table 4.

the commercial treatment applied by the United States and that applied to it by other nations encouraged this protectionist spirit. Latin America has felt the effects of both pressures.

A primary issue in the trade debate between the United States and Latin America concerns access to the U.S. market. This debate is influenced by long-term trends and by short-term pressures related to the severity of the recession. The U.S. market is protected by quotas for numerous Latin American export products (textiles, garments, sugar, beef, and steel). Similarly, the application of U.S. legislation on countervailing duties is an obvious source of tension, particularly with those countries that have not signed the GATT Code of Subsidies.

As already noted, the protection structure in force in the United States discriminates against Latin American exports of manufactured goods and, generally speaking, is higher than the effective protection of the European Economic Community for manufactures (see Table 30). This affects the most dynamic component (excluding oil) of Latin American exports, the component that has the best prospects for future growth.

In all probability, the region will continue to feel the effects of increased U.S. protectionism, which includes new nontariff barriers and is of a sectoral and discriminatory nature. Proposed legislation following the reciprocity principle, under which the United States would demand from its trading counterparts treatment comparable to what it gives, is gaining ground. In the case of developing economies, the application of reciprocity would be accomplished by claiming specific concessions in exchange for those granted by the United States. This approach tends to favor bilateral channels to the detriment of multilateral mechanisms, which governed international trade throughout most of the postwar period. When applied to developing countries, the principle of reciprocity violates the basic criterion that developing nations should be subject to preferential and nonreciprocal treatment.

With regard to U.S. access to the regional market, it is true that the level of protection is much higher in Latin America. It is also true that the restriction on increased U.S. exports to the region is determined by the availability of foreign exchange and not by an import control policy. Because Latin America is a region with external restrictions, this is inevitable. What is under discussion, in any case, is the productive insertion of the region on the international stage and the profile of natural comparative advantages. In the seventies the region increased its imports by dint of a permanently increasing foreign debt, becoming a driving force in international economic growth.

Another issue Latin America will face in the future is the expansion of international trade to include services and direct private investment—particularly when the latter involves international trade in goods. The United States has persistently stated its interest in including services in the international trade rules and regulations. This position was made clear at the GATT ministerial meeting in November 1982. Washington has also declared its decision to grant concessions to developing countries on the basis of reciprocity, including not only trade in goods but also trade in services and the regulation of direct foreign investment.

The graduation concept is at the heart of the debate on trade between the United States and Latin America. In keeping with this principle, the developing countries will be progressively deprived of their preferential access to the U.S. market as their relative level of development improves. Preferential treatment may be negotiated in exchange for a quid pro quo by developing countries. In this case again, the bilateral approach is preferred in the negotiating process. The graduation issue is closely linked to the system of preferences. The U.S. Generalized System of Preferences expires in January 1985, and legislative action is needed to extend or renew it. Initiated in 1976, the GSP allows tax-free entry of about 3,000 products from approximately 140 countries. For the United States, imports covered by the GSP amount to about US $8 billion (3 percent of total U.S. imports). However, for certain beneficiary countries—including some in Latin America—the relative importance is much greater. The significance of the GSP has been reduced since the generalized decline in tariff barriers promoted by GATT. Its extension is considerably limited by the competitive need clause and by the exclusions of the list of sensitive products. The program also discriminates against some countries. Part of the opposition to the GSP in the United States is based on the argument that the program "is more beneficial to the countries which need it least, those which have become more developed and are situated in regions with fewer needs."[1] A central issue, therefore, is the design of graduation mechanisms with respect to the major beneficiaries of the program.

Some have insisted that the GSP and, in general, all systems of preferences have meant more in terms of principle than in effective economic importance. Even if this controversial assertion were correct, in a situation of increasing protectionism the elimination or severe reduction of preferential programs in favor of developing countries could only be interpreted as a new restrictive measure in international trade. Furthermore, it would imply a de facto rejection of the principle systematically promoted by the UN Conference on Trade and Development (UNCTAD) and the developing countries—that the latter need nonreciprocal preferential trade systems for economic and equity reasons. In any case, if preference systems have been of little economic value, one might ask if this has not been precisely the result of their partial, unstable, and discriminatory application by the developed countries. If so, Latin American interests will be better represented by support for the extension of these preferences than by a mere recognition of their present "scant economic value."

Trade is of critical importance in relations between the United States and Latin America, and the areas of conflict and negotiation are many. Perhaps the most significant change in trade relations is in the context within which the decisions of the two parties will be made and future negotiations carried out. The climate of increased liberalization of trade that prevailed during the two and a half decades after the Second World War will most likely be replaced by a climate of restriction and protection of markets more in keeping with the general picture of stagnation that will apparently prevail in the eighties. In this context, the region's need to obtain positive trade balances to cover the repayment and servicing of its accumulated debt will cause increasing difficulties. For this reason, the development and strengthening of a joint negotiating capacity, the continuation and intensification of the trend towards diversification in external economic contacts, and the expansion of the regional integration process constitute the primary and essential lines of action in strengthening the relative position of Latin America.

Latin American–U.S. Financial Relations

During the first year and a half of the Reagan administration's term, financial relations between Latin America and the United States have developed within a general policy framework designed by the new U.S. government. In the second half of 1982, however, some policy changes related to the critical international financial situation occurred.

The clear preference of the Republican administration for market mechanisms (as the most suitable means of regulating international financial links) had to be partially abandoned in face of the critical financial situation of the second half of 1982. The United States not only modified its policy toward the International Monetary Fund; U.S. agencies even assumed an active role in supporting certain critical cases through the provision of "bridge" credits or advances for future purchases. Furthermore, the Reagan administration actively intervened in market mechanisms by informally pressuring private banks—together with the IMF—not to suspend their lines of credit to countries experiencing the greatest difficulties. At least in this case, it was recognized that "market solutions" did not constitute acceptable remedies from the standpoint of the stability of the international financial system.

Financial relations between Latin America and the United States have undergone significant changes over the past two decades. These changes were part of the more general transformation in the international financial market. First, official transfers declined considerably as a percentage of total financing. Second, the percentage of direct investment also declined. Third, the European currency market began to play a much more significant role than national markets in the provision of funds. In other words, a process of increased private participation and "denationalization" of capital flows occurred. These changes had important consequences for financial relations between the United States and Latin America.

Latin America's external debt grew rapidly during the seventies, in particular since the mid-seventies. This debt was concentrated in a handful of countries. High liquidity levels and stagnating production in advanced countries during this period, along with imbalances in the external account resulting from rising oil prices, were decisive operative elements in increasing financial capital flows toward the region. The accelerated rate of debt contraction facilitated the maintenance of relatively high economic growth rates in countries that had felt the adverse effects of the oil-price increase. These countries became an important source of demand for exports from the industrialized countries. In the specific case of trade in manufactures between the United States and Latin America, the favorable U.S. balance grew from US $4 billion in 1970 to US $17.3 billion ten years later.

However, these rates of debt accumulation did not seem sustainable in the long run. Over the last three years, this became more evident through the shortening of the average repayment period and the increase in risk premiums and spreads. These trends led gradually to a situation of extreme liquidity shortage in 1982.

These long-term developments were accelerated and intensified by the economic policy of the United States. The transmission of recessionary conditions from the United States to other national economies meant contraction or slow growth for Latin American export markets. This brought serious consequences for the region, both in terms of export volume and prices. U.S. monetary policy and high interest rates produced a significant increase in the costs of financing and of servicing the cumulative debt (the major part of this contracted at floating interest rates). Moreover, for those

Latin American countries that during the seventies had pursued policies of opening up and integrating their financial sectors into the international market, the depressive and destabilizing effects were multiplied by massive short-term capital outflows. The financial crisis forced the application of highly recessionary programs with a view to restoring some degree of balance to the external sector. The succession of exchange crises and the widespread use of exchange control mechanisms during 1982 clearly reflected the chaotic financial and monetary situation in which most of the economies of the region found themselves.

In 1982, Latin America's balance-of-payments deficit reached an estimated total of US $14 billion, despite the radical turnaround recorded in the merchandise account. The trade balance moved from a deficit of US $600 million in 1981 to a surplus of US $8.8 billion the following year, but the effects of this change were nullified by the increase in net payments of interest and profits, which exceeded US $34 billion—almost double the amount recorded the previous two years. This increase in financial remittances abroad contrasted sharply with the fall in net capital inflows to the region, which declined from US $42 billion in 1981 to US $19.2 billion in 1982.

The impact of the economic policy of the principal industrialized countries—in particular that of the United States—could not have been more devastating. Latin America entered its worst economic crisis since the thirties, a crisis from which no speedy recovery is envisaged. Certainly the handling of domestic economic policy in the region contributed to the severity of the impact. The opening up and integration of financial markets to the world system and the intensive foreign indebtedness became channels for decisive influence on domestic economic processes.

During its first year in office, the Reagan administration reacted to this accumulation of tensions with the international financial policy lines already described above. The emergence of the financial crisis of 1982, together with the suspension of amortization payments by some Latin American countries and the subsequent generalization of this phenomenon at the regional level, clearly reflected the inadequacy and unsuitability of the administration's approach. The reaction of the United States to the 1982 tensions was to change its policy. The Treasury Department, Federal Reserve, and the

Credit Corporation for Primary Products quickly responded by granting "bridge" credits and coordinating support from the Bank for International Settlements while the countries affected were negotiating standby agreements with the International Monetary Fund. These agreements generally included a commitment from the private banks to maintain a flow of resources to these countries, a novel occurrence in the relationship between the IMF and private banks. The process of renegotiating part of the foreign debt of the most affected countries became widespread.

The rescue programs, the renegotiations, and the adjustment programs in progress are unlikely to solve the external debt problem of the Latin American countries. Indeed, some countries are already experiencing problems in meeting their obligations contracted with the International Monetary Fund. Many observers believe this situation will recur with some frequency in the near future, unless the nature of adjustment programs is substantially changed. The likelihood of a new succession of severe external crises such as occurred in the second half of 1982 is not ruled out. If the crisis recurs, the difficulties experienced in 1982 would be considerably multiplied. First, in the most critical cases the IMF has already reached its credit ceiling of 450 percent of the national quota. Second, more intense voluntary participation on the part of the private banks would be unlikely if such emergencies arose.

Meanwhile, the revised U.S. position emphasizes domestic adjustments in terms traditionally proposed by the IMF, pinning hopes on the outcome of the economic recovery now in progress and on the generation of renewed private capital flows. This involves an updating of the principles that originally motivated this policy and that had been partially abandoned in view of the market conditions prevailing in times of crisis. Ths U.S. strategy seems to be based on three assumptions: (1) that the present recovery will be sufficiently concrete and lasting to bring about a substantial improvement in the market conditions for Latin American exports; (2) that adjustment programs presently under way in countries of the region will bring positive results, and more importantly, will be tolerable from a social and political point of view; and (3) that the international financial market is basically in a healthy condition and that private capital flows will be restored in a relatively short time.

The recovery initiated in the first quarter of 1983 seems relatively uncertain, weak, and unstable—too weak to meet the expectations for a significant improvement in the international economy. In addition, the expected maintenance of high unemployment levels will probably keep protectionist pressures high. The imbalances still evident in U.S. fiscal and monetary policy also raise questions concerning future interest rate levels and their effects on the U.S. and world economies. After three years of economic stagnation in the United States, a period of recovery seems almost inevitable. Nevertheless, forecasts as well as effective performance during the first quarter of 1983 leave serious doubts as to the capacity of the economy to turn around the negative trends of the past few years.

Regarding the suitability of adjustment programs now in progress, Latin America has extensive experience in orthodox stabilization programs. There is a relatively broad consensus that these programs produce short-term adjustments in external accounts at a very high domestic economic price. Moreover, the gravity of previous situations in which programs of this nature were applied did not approach the proportions of current external imbalances. The massive accumulation of debts by the economies of the region superimposes an added burden upon the traditional external structural restrictions that have dominated Latin America's economic growth. The debt will require servicing and repayment. This raises serious doubts as to the compatability of traditional programs with the demands of the present crisis. Moreover, there is the question of social and political tolerance of the adjustments required to allow these programs to release resources for repaying and servicing accumulated debt. In the absence of significant new flows of external financial resources (and assuming that markets for Latin American exports will not expand significantly in the near future), adjustments in external accounts will be basically incumbent upon the import account. This does and will continue to have a direct influence on the levels of domestic economic activity and, consequently, on the prevailing indicators of economic well-being. In addition, the types of adjustment that are normally included in stabilization programs now in progress concerning fiscal, pricing, salary, and exchange rate policies have a direct and immediate effect on the country's standard of living.

Finally, the assumption that the private international financial market is in a basically healthy condition and only requires minor adjustments is a hypothesis that at least raises some queries. In the first place, the imbalances in international financial markets are not exclusive to Latin America. The domestic financial markets of industrialized countries—particularly that of the United States—show clear signs of a deterioration in "financial health" over the last few years.[2] This suggests a more generalized level of instability, for which the explanation is to be found in the dynamics of the relatively more important markets. Acceptance of this principle implies that, apart from factors obviously attributable to the economic policies pursued in the last decade, the imbalance has more permanent and deep-rooted causes than mere "irresponsibility" in rates of debt contraction and use of resources.

The risk level accepted by major international banks in relation to certain highly indebted countries greatly limits the possibilities for rapidly reestablishing increased flows of resources to improve the financial standing of these countries. It would be more logical to expect a progressive withdrawal and the maintenance of relations at the level required for continuity in international capital circles. There has been a marked reluctance on the part of smaller banks to continue granting loans to developing countries. In addition, the reservations of large banks with huge external commitments were reflected in the pressures the IMF and the U.S. government exerted to guarantee resource flows that would not interrupt the prevailing delicate "normality."

Without a doubt, renewed external crises in one or a number of countries in Latin America will have an obvious effect on any evaluation of the results obtained from the implementation of adjustment programs in terms of their economic, social, and political costs. At the same time, a general decrease in flexibility in organizing "rescue programs" is likely if these situations recur with some frequency. Apparently, none of these considerations has been taken into account in the Reagan administration's assessment of the present situation. Hence, the political response is not in keeping with the seriousness of the circumstances. Persistent confidence in a market recovery to provide a solution to the present situation seems to bear little relation to foreseeable developments. There is no reason to assume that by the mid-eighties market forces will be in a position to resolve the critical situation generated a decade ago—under more adverse conditions—by its own methods of operation.

The probability that the United States' domestic policy will in itself have a limiting effect on the activity of private banks on the international scene implies the removal of an additional variable that could play an active role in the recovery of international liquidity. At the same time, the level of flexibility in U.S. policy in relation to MDBs seems totally insufficient and inappropriate to meet the demands of this situation.

Conclusions and Recommendations

In the light of the preceding analysis, and bearing in mind Latin America's economic prospects for the next few years, some ideas are submitted below as to how Latin America might approach its future economic relations with the United States.

1. Latin America's relations with the United States, despite many important changes, maintain a basic imbalance associated with the different levels of relative development and the mechanisms and forces that regulate interaction between the various national economies. The region should therefore further diversify its external economic links as a means of increasing its relative bargaining capacity.

2. Present Latin American economic relations with the United States do not require a return to the idea of a "special relationship." In fact, both the region's economic relations and its international policies have been diversified. The region now takes a global approach to its major economic problems. Consequently, the promotion of negotiations with the United States should proceed with due consideration of the interests and positions of the region at the international level.

In this context, it should be remembered that a "special relationship" with Latin America is only envisaged by the United States in times of crisis in the region, or when Washington considers its vital security interests to be at stake. Moreover, the U.S. government entertains the possibility of "special relations" with only some countries or groups of countries in the case of particular critical circumstances, and does not expect to extend this policy to the region as a whole.

3. The medium-term prospects for the U.S. and the world economy are not extremely favorable. Uncertainty still prevails, with doubts as to the stability, prospects, and intensity of the current economic recovery in the United States. Consequently, the countries of Latin America should not base their expectations of an economic revival on an expansion dependent on external factors.

For this reason, Latin America should continue to encourage and intensify the process of regional integration and cooperation by consolidating its respective national economies, and by seeking mechanisms to attenuate the domestic consequences of international economic imbalances. This entails the strengthening of the region's economic security through reciprocal efforts and economic complementarity. The resources that the region itself is able to accumulate and mobilize will be its best guarantee of security in the next few decades, both in terms of its potential future development and its general and bilateral bargaining capacity vis-à-vis the United States.

4. The contradictions between monetary and fiscal policy in the United States had important effects on the U.S. domestic economy and also on the world economy. These effects, felt in both industrialized and developing countries, were transmitted through real and monetary channels. The growth in the levels and inconsistency of real interest rates in the United States and the U.S. decision not to intervene in exchange markets (except in situations of extreme crisis) have had a profoundly destabilizing effect on international monetary markets and speculative capital flows. An additional effect was to increase the burden of foreign debt servicing, with serious repercussions for countries with a high level of indebtedness.

In this regard, it seems advisable for Latin America to promote greater cooperation with other countries and regions adversely affected by U.S. economic policy. The region should emphasize the negative effects of these policies, while pointing out the scant attention paid by the U.S. authorities to the international repercussions of domestic policy. Meetings should be promoted between as many of the affected countries as possible, either in international fora or at the level of regional coordination. These countries should urge international organizations entrusted with the maintenance of the stability of the world monetary and financial system to assume this responsibility.

5. One principle that is already recognized, and on which Latin America should insist in the future, relates to the differences in productive structures and development levels and the resulting consequences for international trade. The granting of generalized preferences addresses this reality. These preferences should therefore be reinforced and expanded in the future. Although the economic significance of these systems has been modest in the past, this is due to their nature and to the way they have been implemented. In the particular case of the U.S. GSP, its partial, unstable, and discriminatory nature has been the cause of its low effective economic value. It is therefore important that the renegotiation of this system, scheduled for 1985, receive special attention by Latin American countries.

6. The growing number of legislative and more general pressures in favor of establishing the principle of reciprocity as the basis of U.S. trade policy should also be closely followed by Latin America. It is highly probable that the policy of granting or maintaining concessions in exchange for privileges will be intensified. In view of this situation, Latin America should reaffirm the need to achieve solutions negotiated at the multilateral level.

7. The United States has made its position clear on the high priority it assigns to the regulation of trade of services, including investment as it relates to trade. Services are a critical area for the region, in view of the repercussions on the development process. Latin America should conduct a thorough analysis of the present situation with regard to trade in services and to the potential effects liberalization of this sector would have on the economies of the region.

8. In the area of finance, relations between Latin America and the United States have undergone substantial modifications, and it is expected that these relations will assume greater importance in the next few years. U.S. authorities acted speedily when a number of imbalances arose in the second half of 1982, but this intervention was casuistic in nature. It was not accompanied by any real changes in the general principles governing that country's economic policy: market and private sector priority and emphasis on recessive adjustments in debtor countries. This approach is clearly inadequate to redress the current structural imbalances.

Latin America should insist on the inadequacy of these partial approaches, but should also bear in mind that its ability to promote other approaches is fundamentally dependent on a greater capacity for concerted action. In this regard, the general type of approach should be intensified as a means of projecting Latin American influence in matters vital to its interests and of counteracting "bilateral" or "regional" initiatives promoted by the United States in response to critical circumstances from the security standpoint.

9. The financial crisis of the early eighties is a shared responsibility. Therefore, the burden of adjustment should be evenly distributed and should not fall, as is the case at present, exclusively on debtor countries. It is clear that the implementation of more equitable and economically less costly adjustment processes will require negotiation at the international level. Without a doubt, such an initiative would undoubtedly include discussions on reforming the international monetary system. U.S. resistance to this initiative will only be modified if sufficient critical mass is achieved in favor of this alternative. In this regard, negotiations and the adoption of common positions with industrialized countries also affected by the present monetary and financial situation are very important. Latin America should stress the need to increase the resources of multilateral financial organizations and to make adjustment conditions more flexible, bearing in mind the need to maintain rates of economic growth that do not involve a deterioration in standards of living.

10. It is also advisable that Latin America insist that the solution to the present economic crisis include the adoption of coordinated economic recovery policies by all members of the international community. In view of the imbalances still existing—at the domestic level in industrialized and developing countries as well as at the international level—the coordination of economic policies and plans seems to be the only option for promoting a lasting and vigorous recovery.

11. Finally, it is important to note that the very nature of the U.S. political system opens the way for the introduction of Latin American positions. The effectiveness of this introduction certainly depends on the level of convergence or divergence of interests. There is, nevertheless, one essential condition for this to be effective: a precise knowledge of how the mechanisms that exert these influences work.[3] In this regard, it would be advisable to establish

a routine review of the state of the U.S. economy and its impact on Latin America.

Notes

1. Senate Hearings on S.1150, *Congressional Record*, 8 May 1981, p. S4643.
2. See H. Kaufman, *National Policies and the Deteriorating Balance Sheets of Corporations* (New York: Solomon Brothers, 1981).
3. See "The Complexities of U.S. Foreign Policy and National Interest" in the Annex of this volume, which analyzes aspects of the U.S. decision-making process.

Annex—U.S. Foreign Policy and the Economy: Decision Making and Levels of Negotiation

The Complexities of U.S.
Foreign Policy and National Interest

One of the fundamental characteristics of U.S. foreign policy since the Second World War has been the complexity of the various specialized levels at which it is formulated. U.S. policymaking has involved the increasing participation of a growing number of agencies, departments, coordinating councils, and other institutional bodies. The process of shaping pluralist and decentralized decision-making mechanisms has allowed a variety of agents to influence the final results.

Until the Second World War, U.S. foreign policymaking was a coherent and centralized process. The competent organ for its formulation was unquestionably the State Department. Diplomatic style and interests were a major factor in the determination of this policy, and the criteria involved served as the basis for coordinating different areas. This meant, in effect, that if an economic or military problem having implications for foreign policy arose, it was automatically transferred to the State Department. Final decisions were almost always made between the State Department and the White House, generally without the intervention of other agencies.

The growth in the power and productive capacity of the United States at the end of the Second World War completely changed this pattern. Foreign policy became a complex matter involving many different, specialized spheres of international concern, each governed by its own set of rules. No longer the central focus, foreign policy diplomacy became merely one of several determinants of the United States' international conduct. Emerging factors that rapidly acquired major significance included international military policy, international security and intelligence policy, international policy governing the entry of foreign labor, and especially international economic policy.

Areas of complementarity and conflict were established at all levels. Specialized technical teams sought to impose their views in the conduct of foreign policy. On a number of borderline issues, bitter disputes arose as to who held final responsibility. But at times these specialized agencies, united by bureaucratic interests, took a joint stand vis-à-vis political teams that enjoyed more direct access to the president, causing bitter rivalries. U.S. foreign policy moved from consensus and continuity to become an area of conflictive proposals and continual political arbitration over the frequent disparities created by a huge administrative machinery possessing substantial resources.

In the midst of this plurality of views and interests, the various sectors involved in the formulation of foreign policy finally agreed on the need for a common authority. This was made easier by the gradual abandonment of the original ideological-ethical tradition of U.S. foreign policy, which at the birth of the nation and during its early stages of development regarded international activity as an instrument to promote the dissemination of the values and guidelines of U.S. democracy throughout the world. Once this aim was replaced by a policy based on power, it became possible to organize U.S. international affairs around the objectives of "national interest." Thus, the enhancement of the nation's power began to bear a direct relationship to the preservation and development of U.S. national interests. This, in turn, was seen as a concept subject to dynamic changes, requiring readjustment whenever the prevailing international economic or political conditions changed.

In the mid-fifties, Walt Rostow gave a definition of U.S. national interest that had a great impact at the time and which, in view of its present-day relevance, it is timely to recall. Rostow stated:

U.S. interest resides in the maintenance of a world environment for the United States within which American society can continue to develop in accordance with the humanistic principles on which it is founded. In terms of the progressive development of the quality of U.S. society, this definition includes not only the physical protection of the country but also the protection of a way of life which is still evolving.

The operative significance of this definition stems from the geographical location of the United States. The interests of the United States have never been automatically ensured by virtue of geographical isolation for any significant length of time in the nation's history. Contrary to a myth still strongly influencing American attitudes and the country's line of action, United States interests have been in chronic danger from the end of the eighteenth century onwards. This danger arose and continues to arise for the simple geographical reason that the combined resources of Eurasia, including military might, have been and continue to be superior to that of the United States, Eurasia being understood to be Asia, the Middle East, Africa and Europe.[1]

We can conclude from the foregoing that the concept of national interest which has become the focal point in the formulation of all the United States' contemporary foreign policy, involves two complementary objectives: the search for material and physical security conditions for the state and U.S. society, and an overall correlation of political forces allowing for the reproduction of liberal-democratic values and principles of organization prevailing in the United States.

These objectives show the clear influence of President Franklin D. Roosevelt's international ideas. During the thirties Roosevelt had to carry the burden of the last stage of predominantly isolationist international thinking in the history of the United States. The three Republican presidents of the twenties—Harding, Coolidge, and Hoover—asserted the need for U.S. military withdrawal, partly as compensation for Washington's failure to impose its conditions in the peace treaties that followed the First World War. Even more important was the conviction that an introverted attitude was necessary to maintain the conditions of prosperity and economic growth typical of that period of U.S. history. Roosevelt chose instead to involve the United States openly in world conflicts. He believed that active participation in the defeat of the Axis countries and in support of world democracy would enable his country to bring about a historical shift in the balance of power from European to extra-European hegemony, and more concretely towards U.S. hegemony.

The concept of national interest as the most decisive element in the formulation of U.S. foreign policy quickly took hold. It received support from distinguished U.S. experts on international relations such as Hans Morgenthau, George Kennan, and Robert Osgood. The idea that the United States should organize its international affairs in a realistic and pragmatic way was raised to the level of an unquestionable principle by these specialists. The national aim was for the United States to increase its share of power within the various entities comprising the international community, and to enhance the United States' position in the different regions of the world. These ideas had a profound influence on the Cold War policy and the bipolar confrontation of the superpowers—the United States and the Soviet Union—that characterized the entire immediate postwar period. Despite adjustments, this view of U.S. national interest continues to dominate the entire formulation of foreign policy.

The Levels of U.S. Foreign Policy–Making and Their Impact on U.S. Bargaining Power

The formulation of the United States' international economic policy is affected by the levels at which U.S. policy is determined. This is important because the decisions made within a more general or a more specific context set the stage for negotiations between the various foreign states and governments with Washington.

This factor became more complex and sophisticated in the seventies. Following the Second World War, the United States formulated its foreign policy at three levels: global, regional, and bilateral. The regional level was the central theme in almost all announcements of new policies; bilateral relations dominated the more operative and routine areas. Infrequent global approaches were reserved for specific issues.

The decline of U.S. hegemony imposed a considerable number of readjustments in the formulation of U.S. foreign policy. U.S. diplomacy had to contend with a series of new phenomena that emerged from the changes perceived in the balance of power between major powers, and especially in relations with the United States. The two most important trends were the increasing international presence of the Third World (both through the Group of 77 and the nonaligned movement), which initiated what was termed in the United States the "politicization" of debates in international organizations; and increasing international activity on the part of the EEC countries and Japan. These countries began to pursue a much more active policy vis-à-vis the developing world, making proposals that were no longer concerted or coordinated with the United States in the areas of politics, trade, investment, and the transfer of technology. These circumstances caused a total reorganization of the rationale and content of the foreign policy decision-making process in the United States. Latin America was proposed as the first area in which this process would be restructured.

In 1974 Roger Hansen of the Overseas Development Council made a study of the different areas in which the United States should respond to its new international challenges. This study, undertaken in preparation for the first Linowitz report,[2] sparked an extensive debate on foreign policy that has profoundly influenced the action pursued by recent U.S. administrations in Latin America. The basic issues concerned the validity of regional policies and the desirability of joint strategies for conducting negotiations with the Third World. An alternative was to dissolve the bloc of developing countries and organize a group of countries whose views were more in keeping with U.S. interests. The prevailing criterion was that regional identification had ceased to constitute an adequate point of reference for U.S. policy, because the different levels of development attained by the countries involved had widened the gap between them.

The State Department was directed to design an appropriate classification of Third World countries according to their relative levels of development. This implied the definition of different criteria for the most backward countries ("desperately poor," in the language of the State Department); for nations that have reached an intermediate stage in the process of modernization but have not yet attained a definite industrial base; and for the "emerging powers"— those countries possessing positive factors such as an important demographic base, raw materials or energy resources, regional military power, or other capabilities that make them natural regional leaders and place them closer to the circle of industrial nations.[3]

Policy recommendations that were widely supported toward the end of the administration of President Gerald Ford specifically advised that these criteria be used in defining a new policy toward Latin America. Despite variations in the substance of U.S. policy toward Latin America, these new criteria were still based on the four fundamental levels of foreign policy: global, regional, subregional, and bilateral.

The global level refers to the formation of a set of uniform criteria concerning different issues to serve as a basis for U.S. policy organization in relation to the Third World. There are two major concerns at this level. The first is to formulate integrated policies on matters of foreign aid, trade, arms sales, transfer of technology, nonproliferation of nuclear weapons, human rights, and similar issues. In theory, the criteria defined in these policies—which should be special and complementary in nature—would serve as a frame of reference for defining the treatment and negotiations with the entire developed world. The second concern is to develop a policy of special treatment for emerging middle powers. The main criterion has been to introduce mechanisms for preferential discussions and negotiations with a small circle of countries considered to be Third World leaders. The United States should seek to improve relations and, if possible, conclude special agreements with these emerging powers.

The basic aim in identifying countries subject to "a special relationship" was to single them out from their immediate surroundings. If the United States were to establish certain common criteria with the most influential governments in different regions through preferential bilateral agreements, then the adjustment process with the remainder of the area would, theoretically, be facilitated. For this purpose the State Department had made careful estimates of the effects of these powers on the gross national

product, the population, strategic energy reserves, and other resources of each region.

The U.S. government has persistently sought to make this system
work in the past few years. The first systematic attempt to implement
this policy was made at the fourth UNCTAD meeting in Nairobi,
Kenya, in 1976.[4] U.S. Secretary of State Henry Kissinger proposed
a new platform based, for the first time, on the assumption that
negotiations with developing countries were inevitable. His proposal
recommended seeking an agreement on raw materials, and also
offered to create an international bank to act as an intermediary
between private capital and the states receiving investments. In
exceptional circumstances, this bank could serve as a mechanism
for stabilizing the international price of raw materials.

Although U.S. foreign policy has not achieved notable success
at the global level, this level has consistently been the highest
priority for the U.S. government. Under the Carter administration,
globalism was associated with the concern for global management
and issues of international political legitimacy proposed as part of
the trilateral strategy. Under the Reagan administration, the formulation of foreign policy has been dominated by East-West considerations. Yet despite the difference in content, the method of
formulating policy has remained constant.

This explains the bankruptcy of regional policy toward Latin
America under the last two U.S. administrations. The transfer of
issues and countries to the realm of global definition and the
preference for certain subregional systems have detracted from the
importance of what was formerly referred to in Washington as
inter-American policy. The view that the whole of Latin America
could be treated as a more or less homogeneous region is no longer
supported by those responsible for formulating U.S. foreign policy.

For that reason, homogeneity between certain groups of countries
has been sought at the subregional level—which now occupies the
important place assigned to regionalism in previous decades. The
United States does not consider Latin America, now or potentially,
as an integrated unit in international negotiation. A review of all
activities undertaken by Washington in recent years confirms the
consistency of this viewpoint.

Finally, there is the bilateral level, the level of the permanent
and traditional work in the diplomatic conduct of any state. In the

United States, bilateralism has been the sphere preferred by Republican administrations, and it remains an area with great possibilities for action by the State Department's professional bureaucracy. This explains why these two sectors—the State Department and Republicans—have historically been the most insistent on disaggregated action, even to the point of giving primacy to the differences from country to country. They have stressed the opportunities their more specialized knowledge offers the area's dominant power in successfully concluding a separate economic and political arrangement with each country.

The Reagan administration has implemented a Latin American policy to complement its strategic globalism, while actively handling bilateral relations. It has given special attention to certain subregions most seriously affected by political crises, in particular Central America and the Caribbean, which have been grouped together in the Caribbean Basin Initiative. In making proposals to the United States, or in negotiating with Washington, it is very important that Latin America bear in mind the Republican government's policy of differentiating between the various areas. This prevents Latin America from being treated as a regional political bloc with common platforms and interests to discuss and adjust with Washington.

To date, Latin American governments have adopted the same terms of reference as the United States with regard to their policies concerning international economic questions, although their content has of course been adapted to their own interests. They were in the forefront of global negotiation efforts through the North-South dialogue, and they made several unsuccessful attempts in multilateral permanent organizations, such as UNCTAD and UNIDO (UN Industrial Development Organization) to revive the old systems of cooperation in specific fields. They have also promoted a number of formulas for bilateral relations.

Following the South Atlantic conflict between Great Britain and Argentina over the Falklands (Malvinas), there have been repeated discussions on possible forms of a "Latin American reidentification" among many countries in the region. This concept returns to the idea of a Latin America with common interests, willing, as such, to enter into a dialogue with the United States. This would constitute a first step toward persuading the U.S. government to adopt a positive position in its relations to Latin America, departing from the traditional U.S. position. This effort will require careful attention to tactics and content in order to achieve a favorable result.

Latin America's solidarity in the face of U.S. pressures on Argentina or, more recently, on Nicaragua has set the stage for a new approach to Latin American–U.S. relations.

The Growing Importance and Diversification of U.S. International Economic Policy

One of the most important elements in U.S. international affairs since the Second World War has been the constantly increasing importance of its international economic policy. We have seen that up to 1945 this policy was merely a complementary and subordinate chapter in U.S. diplomatic strategy. However, the new responsibilities assumed by Washington upon becoming the leading force in the capitalist bloc quickly shifted priority to economic issues. Stephen Cohen has pointed out that "international economic policy is a child of the Second World War, born of the Bretton Woods Agreements."[5]

Thus the United States, which had rarely participated in international economic negotiations promoted by European states (economic history texts mention Washington's interest and participation in the 1934 London economic conference as an exception), now became the true director of world economic affairs. Its domestic decisions set the norms for several states, or at least had a decisive effect on their behavior. These new responsibilities forced the U.S. government to specialize in various areas of foreign economic policy in order to cover the specialized requirements and demands of this new area of policy and negotiation.

Because of these demands, the subsystem that includes the decision-making process and the content of international economic policy became one of the most extensive and complex in the United States. U.S. global economic activity has become increasingly important in the last forty years, and the growing difficulties of the U.S. economy in the foreign sector have also demanded that greater attention be paid to this sector. The number of institutions involved in the formation of international economic policy has increased correspondingly.[6] To give a clear picture of the various areas of economic policy, we will analyze them separately.

Trade Policy

U.S. international trade policy in the eighties is based on the system of free trade. Those who manage exports and imports in the United States believe an open economy and the smooth exchange of goods and services is the best way of fulfilling their task. With its foreign trade amounting to approximately 9 percent of GNP and representing 20 percent of the country's entire production, the United States is one of the developed economies least dependent on foreign trade.[7] However, due to the volume and value of U.S. production, this trade continues to have a decisive impact on domestic U.S. productive processes and on the margins of economic maneuverability of many other countries of the world.

The situation has been complicated for foreign policy–makers in Washington since the decline in some of the nation's traditional industrial branches has led to a loss of domestic and foreign markets for their products. This trade recession has led to protectionist pressure. The great effectiveness of lobbying by producer organizations in areas such as textiles, footwear, and certain agricultural products has generated one of the most complex adjustment processes in U.S. government in recent years. On the one hand, the affected interest groups lobby for trade barriers, while on the other hand, the administrators of foreign trade policy try with difficulty to defend the principles of free trade.

All three branches of the U.S. government have been involved in these processes. The executive branch has the power to facilitate or hinder the inflow of goods and services from abroad (especially when this flow has recently been associated with the increased participation of Japan and the NICs), making its decisions the basis for the policy adoption process. The legislature has the authority to ratify rules and regulations safeguarding the interests of local producers. The judiciary branch includes the rulings of the Supreme Court, which on many occasions has had to annul the rights of entry of certain products to the U.S. market. Some of the more well known cases have involved Brazilian footwear and Mexican tomatoes.

For Latin American countries, a knowledge of the decision-making circuit of U.S. international trade policy is highly important. This comprises several government and administration units headed by the Department of Commerce.[8] Within the department, which is basically responsible for the promotion of U.S. foreign trade, there are three units that assist the Secretary of Commerce in defining policy. The International Trade Administration is the part of the Under-Secretariat of International Trade in charge of strengthening the U.S. position in international trade and investment, by creating favorable conditions for placing U.S. goods and services in foreign markets and determining the conditions for the entry of imported goods. The National Technical Information Service, which is responsible for the transfer of technology, promotes the dissemination of U.S. technology abroad and informs U.S. producers of foreign technology. Finally, there is the Bureau of Industrial Economics, which is responsible for monitoring overall industrial development and keeping the government and businessmen informed of same.

Together with the centralized efforts of the Commerce Department, it is increasingly important to bear in mind the work of the Office of the U.S. Trade Representative. This agency, located within the Office of the President at the White House, was created in 1963 by President Kennedy, who foresaw the need for more effective coordination in foreign trade after the convening of the first UNCTAD meeting in Geneva in 1964. Since then, this office has expanded its field of activity. Its current duties include participation in the establishment of U.S. trade policy; coordination of U.S. action in GATT and UNCTAD; coordination of U.S. positions and negotiations vis-à-vis the OECD; handling of all negotiations dealing with the operation of the raw materials market; responsibility for bilateral and multilateral trade negotiations including the criteria for East-West trade; and the establishment of U.S. negotiating platforms in practically all the international economic conferences the government participates in.

Agricultural Policy

Due to the vast volume of its agricultural surplus, the United States is a major force in world food supply. In recent years food products have been scarce, especially in several Third World countries. For this reason, in the seventies, several U.S. foreign policy–makers considered the possibility of counterbalancing U.S. shortfalls in energy with its "food strength." Since the days of Earl Butz, secretary of agriculture under President Ford, "food as a weapon" has been under discussion.[9]

The powerful Midwest farmers who generate the bulk of grain production in the United States are greatly interested in state support in seeking rapid outlets for their products. They oppose the use of food as a U.S. diplomatic weapon, as was the case in early 1980 when President Carter decreed an embargo on the sale of grain to the USSR as a reprisal against the Soviet military presence in Afghanistan. To give an idea of the strength and influence of U.S. agricultural export circles: In 1981, agricultural exports were valued at US $47 billion and represented one of the most positive areas in the U.S. balance of trade.

The management of U.S. international agricultural policy thus fluctuates between two contradictory poles: on the one hand, placing food and agricultural inputs at the service of a political and diplomatic strategy; on the other, championing the interests of large-scale producers by placing state activities at the service of marketing surplus production with no political restrictions. Defining this foreign policy is mainly the responsibility of the Department of Agriculture, where different internal units specialize in the various problems raised by the external projection of the country's agricultural strength. For some decades now the official tasks of the Department of Agriculture have included facilitating the export of U.S. agricultural products to foreign markets through the complementary activity of four separate agencies. First is the Foreign Agricultural Service, which handles the promotion of U.S. agricultural products in foreign markets by establishing agreements for their placement and sale. This unit is in charge of an international system of agricultural intelligence comprising 100 agricultural experts who calculate future crops and markets for various products in 100 countries and give periodic reports for the benefit and information of U.S. farmers. Second is the Commodity Credit Corporation, which is responsible for advancing resources to farmers and channeling food to foreign aid programs, particularly the PL 480 and Food for Peace programs. The Office of International Cooperation and Development, which is responsible for international development of technical cooperation in the areas of food and agriculture, offering aid agreements to U.S. allied countries, is the third agency; the World Food and Agricultural Outlook and Situation

Board, which systematically keeps track of markets for agricultural products, determines the prices for various products, and submits periodical information to local producers, is the fourth.

Energy

Another area of specialized interest in U.S. international economic policy is energy. Despite the fact that the country has a much higher degree of autonomy in energy than other industrialized countries, this problem was assigned top priority in the past decade. The growth trend in domestic consumption, together with the depletion of domestic sources, made energy one of the main areas of future potential vulnerability for U.S. power.

Since the Yom Kippur war of October 1973 and the embargo decreed by the members of the Organization of Arab Petroleum Exporting Countries against the United States, concern over ensuring the supplies of oil and gas required by the U.S. economy has been extremely important. In 1975, Secretary of State Kissinger admitted the existence of contingency plans for an eventual military occupation of Saudi Arabia or other, smaller Middle Eastern countries possessing large energy reserves. In 1979, the formation of the Rapid Deployment Force was clearly associated with that type of mission, which is still on the present administration's list of priorities. This development links energy problems more directly to issues of strategy and national security.

The management of energy policy, both domestic and foreign, led President Carter to create the Department of Energy (DOE) in 1977. This department is in charge of all aspects of energy; it administers a broad policy to balance the sources of domestic energy with external supplies, reduce U.S. dependence on foreign energy sources, promote the development of new technologies in this area, encourage the application of energy conservation programs, regulate production conditions and the use of alternative energy sources in the United States, and supervise the development of nuclear arms programs. These complex aims have made the Department of Energy a bureaucratic center with one of the largest concentrations of experts and technicians on its staff.

One of the most involved aspects of the work of the DOE is the relationship it maintains with powerful U.S. oil companies, whose transnational activities to a large extent condition world energy market operations. Consequently, most of the actions involved in the coordination of this department's external activities are the result of previous coordination with major producers of the private sector.

The Department of Energy has a special office for international affairs, managed by an assistant secretary for international affairs. This office is responsible for formulating a policy on the safe transport of energy; conducting in-depth studies of oil markets, with special concern for the changes in price trends and for the productive capacity of the various oil-exporting states; considering various international proposals, including the national energy policy plan the President is expected to submit to Congress every two years for consideration; and managing negotiations with the governments of those countries important in the field of energy. The negotiations are to ensure that these countries meet the production required by consumer countries and also implement the policy on nuclear nonproliferation that is of such vital interest to the United States.

The area of international energy policy thus seems to involve many more internal consensual elements than do other specialized areas of U.S. international economic policy. In this area, the main interests of large U.S. enterprises, the government, and consumers coincide almost completely with respect to the international aspects of an energy strategy.

Transportation

In the twenties, the most vigorous growth in the industrial power of the United States was associated with the expansion of the automobile industry, and the United States also had a head start in the aeronautical industry. As a result, the major U.S. producers of transportation services became very influential; they were often capable of mobilizing the public authorities in support of their needs at the international level.

This joining of forces to gain support has intensified as a result of challenges from foreign producers against U.S. consortia in areas such as the automobile industry, where national production has been displaced on the domestic market itself. In these circumstances, the support of Washington has become vital to automobile manufacturers, for the protection of the U.S. industry's share in the world market and also in the U.S. domestic market. This support is coordinated by an assistant secretary for policy and international affairs, whose functions have been gaining importance in the Department of Transportation.

The implementation of international transportation policy has involved arduous trade battles. The department is engaged in negotiations with the Japanese government for a "voluntary" reduction in quotas for vehicles sent to the United States, and in efforts to assist manufacturers of both passenger and military aircraft in placing their products on foreign markets, preferably in developing countries. Negotiations are also under way to create conditions for a program of technical innovation enabling the transportation sector to recover its competitiveness. These issues have made the area of transportation, which had practically no autonomy at the time the Transportation Department was created in 1966, a top priority sector today.

Credit and Financial Policy

Finally, credit and financial policy, whose management is largely the responsibility of the Department of the Treasury, may also be considered a high priority sector in the international economic policy of the United States. The treasury traditionally takes the lead in the formulation of all U.S. economic policies, without prejudice to other entities in handling specialized problems.

Financial issues have taken on new importance since the administration of President Richard Nixon made an about-face in August 1971. Since then, the United States' international agenda has included a set of unresolved financial issues. These include the reorganization of the international monetary system to ensure a position favorable to the dollar; adequate coordination of actions between the U.S. government and the international financial community; and more recently, the management of the foreign debts of Third World countries, especially those intermediate-level countries that had privileged access to the financial liquidity typical of the seventies.

The Treasury Department is organized like a large "engine room" in which some of the most crucial aspects of U.S. global economic activity are concentrated. In no other department—except perhaps the State Department—is such importance attached to international affairs. U.S. international financial policies are formulated by committees of representatives of various agencies. These committees necessarily include representatives from various administrative bodies, as there are usually two or more agencies that claim authority over the same matter.

International financial policies are drafted by three different intergovernmental committees, all headed by the Treasury Department. The committee covering the widest subject area is the Senior Interdepartmental Committee for International Economic Policy, created by Secretary of State George Schultz in July 1982. This committee operates within the framework of the National Security Council and includes cabinet-level representatives of the Departments of the Treasury, State, Defense, Commerce; the Office of Management and Budget; the Central Intelligence Agency; the National Security Council; the Council of Economic Advisors; and the Office of the President. The International Monetary Group operates at the under-secretary level from the Departments of State and Treasury, the Board of the Federal Reserve, and the Council of Economic Advisors. The National Advisory Council on International Monetary and Financial Policies, created in 1945 to coordinate U.S. policies vis-à-vis the IMF and the World Bank, has lost much of its original importance since then.

In structural terms, the secretary of the treasury acts as coordinator of the Economic Policy Group, a ministerial body that coordinates all the administration's economic actions and officially defines U.S. positions in the main international economic organizations—the IMF, the World Bank, and the regional development banks (Inter-American, African, and Asian). The assistant secretary for international affairs and the under-secretary for monetary affairs are concerned with aspects critical to U.S. international positions: the definition of policies on investment abroad, aid programs for developing countries, international proposals on monetary restructuring, relations with developed countries concerning joint efforts in the areas of production and industry. They also coordinate the specialized policies already described in the areas of commerce, energy, transportation, and agriculture.

The leading role that the Treasury Department plays in international economic policy also involves a relationship with several nondepartment economic organizations that are of great importance in defining U.S. world strategies. They include the Federal Reserve Board, which operates at such a high level of autonomy that it resembles a sui generis central bank; the Council of Economic Advisors, in the Office of the President; the Agency for International Development, in the Department of State; and the Overseas Private Investment Corporation. These are only a few of the economic bodies participating in the decision-making chain in this area. They often take an active role in defining policies affecting either some Latin American countries or the region as a whole.

The Role of Congress

Congress has not played an active role in the more specialized aspects of international financial and monetary matters such as exchange control. It intervenes much more in the area of international financial agencies, as Congress must approve U.S. contributions.

Financing for multilateral development banks, like other government expenditure, has to be applied for by the executive branch. Congress is responsible for authorization and the allocation of resources. Financing for MDBs is included in the general budget resolution (under the foreign business section) that must be approved and sanctioned annually by Congress. Resources for MDBs need to be approved once every three or four years, depending on the specific institution and the duration of U.S. commitment.

In the House of Representatives, MDB authorizations fall within the jurisdiction of the international development, institutes, and finance subcommittee of the House Committee on Banking, Finance and Urban Affairs. This subcommittee gives a series of hearings, followed by a "mark-up"—the session in which it decides whether to approve the application, increase or reduce the budget, or reject the application outright. After the mark-up, the draft bill passes to the banking committee, which does its own mark-up to approve, disapprove, or modify the action of the subcommittee. The draft then passes to the standards committee, which determines the rules of procedure governing the debate of the draft in the House, which meets in a plenary session to approve it (frequently with amendments) or reject it.

In the Senate, the executive's application is directly discussed in a plenary session of the subcommittee for foreign affairs. It is then submitted to the consideration of the full Senate. If the application is approved by the Senate and the House, any differences in the two versions are adjusted in a committee comprising members of the Senate and the House. The draft submitted by this committee must then be approved by the House and the Senate. If approved, it passes to the president, who either approves and signs the draft (in which case it becomes law) or vetoes it.

In obtaining MDB financing, the authorization procedure is only the first step, as the money must also be authorized and allocated. The administration's application for "allocation" is submitted to the allocations committees of the House and the Senate, which in turn send it to their respective subcommittees on foreign operations. Usually, the House acts first: There are hearings, a mark-up by a subcommittee, another by a plenary committee meeting, action by the standards committee, and then action taken in a plenary session of the House. Once the draft bill is approved in the House, it usually goes through another mark-up by the Senate Subcommittee on Foreign Operations; then it is passed to a plenary commission meeting, followed by a Senate plenary session. If necessary, adjustments are made by a joint committee of the Senate and the House.

It should also be noted that in approving financing for MDBs, Congress always acts after the U.S. administration has already committed itself to a certain level of contributions. Here there are certain dichotomies. In the U.S. system, Congress is different from the executive power from the functional point of view. The congressional committees, particularly the allocations committees, consider it their duty to save money by reducing the amounts requested by the executive branch in various areas. For this reason, no "commitment" assumed by the administration in an international conference is binding. Congress is under no legal obligation to fulfill this type of international commitment. It is for this reason that U.S. financing of international organizations has historically led to political conflicts within Congress and between Congress and the executive branch.

Increases in the IMF quotas also have to be authorized and allocated, although U.S. contributions are not considered expenditure for budgetary purposes. In the House, the banking subcommittee on international trade, investment, and monetary policy has initial authorization jurisdiction. The draft then follows the same route as authorization for the MDBs. In the Senate, initial authorization jurisdiction is shared between the foreign affairs committee and the subcommittee for international monetary and financial policy, which is a subcommittee of the Senate Committee for Urban Affairs, Housing and Banking.

The appropriations process for draft legislation is exactly the same for the IMF as for the MDBs. The main legislative anomaly concerning MDB and IMF financing is that the House Committee on Foreign Affairs plays no part in authorization, whereas the Senate Committee on Foreign Affairs plays an active role in both cases.

Conclusions

The most important point in this review, for anyone concerned with the origin and formulation of U.S. international economic policy, or for anyone conducting negotiations for which the background decision-making process is decisive, is that in every given situation it is essential to identify the particular "circuit" that affects government agreements. This enables the negotiator to recognize which institutions have a role to play in the policy line adopted, and to identify the economic groups and private interests that have been lobbying to influence the decision.

For a long time, all aspects of the operating mechanisms for U.S. policy definition and decision making were little known. In the seventies, however, a series of analyses that consolidated a trend in the study of U.S. international relations—the bureaucratic approach—helped to clarify the steps, processes, and levels of decision-making in the area of international economic policy. These efforts were reinforced in 1975 with the creation of the Committee on the Organization of Government for the Conduct of Foreign Policy. This committee, in collaboration with the most prominent experts in the academic community, produced seven volumes of analysis on the overall aspects of the issue and several case studies. The published documents, known as the *Murphy Report*, supply a substantial amount of information that facilitates a more precise study of this subject.[10]

A significant initiative that could be taken in Latin America in the near future, with a view to acquiring greater knowledge of the

United States and increasing the region's bargaining power vis-à-vis that country, would be to identify certain central issues for the continent, follow them up within the context of the U.S. state machinery (executive and Congress), and thus make possible a timely presentation of Latin American criteria regarding these problems. By acquiring a greater knowledge of the U.S. bureaucracy, the region could thus increase its bargaining power vis-à-vis the United States.

It should be borne in mind that in the area of international economic policy, some variables of general interest are also applicable. These are adequately established in general studies on decision making. The main criteria are:

1. *Each issue or country is of variable significance depending on the extent to which it affects the U.S. national interest at any given moment.* Consequently, in any analysis it is essential to distinguish between the decision-making process in times of crisis and the routine or normal process. The more a problem is perceived as directly influencing the strategic interests of the United States, the higher the rank of the officials entrusted with its solution.

Under normal conditions, the majority of issues of interest to Latin American countries receive low-level treatment. This implies the possibility of great disparity and conflict between the various bureaucratic groups influencing the decision to be made. When the matter is situated within a context of crisis, decisions tend to be centralized, the issue is dealt with at a higher level, and the decision-making process approximates the model described by Graham Allison as the "unified rational actor."[11] This variability in the treatment of various concerns makes it crucial to identify the relative importance of an issue at every step of the way.

2. *Growing subject specialization exists in the formulation of U.S. foreign policy.* Instead of a single, unified foreign policy, nowadays there are different specialized international policies. This gives rise to networks of connections or preferential relations, of a rather permanent nature, between certain private groups having foreign interests and specific bureaucratic circles. This specialization of pressure groups is seen both in departments and agencies of the executive branch and in the subcommittees and committees of the two houses. From the methodological point of view, one can study

the relationship in accordance with the rules of the "clientele" system. The specialized professional bureaucracies cater to the demands of certain interest groups because they believe that a helpful attitude toward them strengthens their respective political positions.[12]

3. *There are many different interests among the political bodies connected with the executive and bureaucratic groups.* The "doctrines" and "theories" on which career officials base their interpretation of U.S. national interest tend to be rather stable, regardless of the issue involved. Because these ideas are frequently in conflict with the political views of officials entering with a new administration, there is a marked tendency towards conflict and disagreement. Similarly, it can be concluded that when political teams are unable to obtain the direct support of the White House for their criteria, the positions sustained by the administrative nuclei will form the prevailing norm.

4. *The "political time" for the implementation of presidential programs is limited.* Every new administration arrives at the White House with a significant amount of political power. The period of greatest power is during the months following the change of administrations. During this "honeymoon," Congress establishes a truce to support the projects of the new president; the press tends to be indulgent with the president's programs; and in general, it is thought that the president has a right to implement his programs. By and large, this period lasts for the entire first year of a new administration, after which political control becomes stricter, control mechanisms operate more effectively, and the press and mass media begin to examine the occupant of the White House more critically.

Because of this honeymoon effect, most of the important and successful initiatives that an administration can make are those proposed at the beginning of its mandate. A program of great importance, particularly if it implies significant adjustments or modifications in the social sectors or economic groups, generally has less chance for approval during the second half of the administration. This modification in the balance of power is furthered by the congressional election that occurs two years after a presidential election and serves to test the strength of the government. The president usually loses a part of his legislative support, forcing him to adopt a more open and compromising attitude toward Congress.

Notes

1. See Walt W. Rostow, *Los Estados Unidos en la palestra mundial* (Madrid: Editorial Tecnos, 1962), p. 579.

2. See Roger Hansen, *U.S. Latin American Economic Policy: Bilateral, Regional, or Global?* Overseas Development Council, Development Paper no. 18, Washington, D.C., 1975.

3. Over the past few years, an important trend has developed toward analyzing the issue of medium and emerging powers. Among others, the following texts may be consulted: Eric Hanson, "The Economic Policies of Middle Power," in J. King Gordon, ed., *Canada's Role as a Middle Power* (Toronto: Canadian Institute of International Affairs, 1965); Paul Painchaud, "Middle-Powermanship as an Ideology," in Gordon, *Canada's Role*; Carsten Holbraad, *The Role of Middle Powers*, School of International Affairs Occasional Papers, Carleton University, Ottawa, Canada, 1962; Leopoldo González Aguayo, "Aproximación a una teoría de las potencias medianas," *Relaciones Internacionales* 2, 8 (January-March 1975); David A. Baldwin, "Power Analysis and World Politics: New Trend Versus Old Tendencies," *World Politics* 31, 2 (January 1979); Peter Worsley, "Un mundo o tres? Concepciones del Tercer Mundo," (CIDE, Mexico, 1982, mimeo.); Friedrich Kratochwil, "On the Notion of Interest in International Relations," *International Organization* 36, 1 (Winter 1982); and Guadalupe González, "Dilemas y perspectivas de una potencia media regional: Las nuevas dimensiones de la política exterior Mexicana" (CIDE, Mexico, 1982, mimeo.).

4. See *Estados Unidos Perspectiva Latinoamericana* 1, 1 (August 1976, CIDE, Mexico).

5. See Stephen Cohen, *The Making of United States International Foreign Policy*, 2d ed. (New York: Praeger Publishers, 1981), p. 7.

6. On the making of U.S. international policy, especially see Stephen Cohen and Ronald Meltzer, *United States International Economic Policy in Action* (New York: Praeger Publishers, 1982); Cohen, *Making of United States Policy*; and Robert Pastor, *Congress and the Politics of U.S. Foreign Economic Policy, 1929–1976* (Berkeley: University of California Press, 1980).

7. See the address by Ambassador William E. Brock before the National Press Club, 18 May 1982 (telex).

8. The information in this section has basically been taken from *The United States Government Manual 1981-1982*, published by the Office of the Federal Register, National Archives and Records Service, General Services Administration (Washington, D.C.: GPO, 1981).

9. See Mirta Botzman, "El uso de los alimentos en la política exterior norteamericana: El embargo de granos en la Union Soviética," *Cuaderno Semestral de Estados Unidos*, no. 12 (1982, CIDE, Mexico).

10. See Committee on the Organization of Government for the Conduct of Foreign Policy, *Murphy Report*, especially vol. 3, *Case Studies on U.S. Foreign Economic Policy, 1965–74, and Conduct of Routine Economic Relations* (Washington, D.C.: GPO, 1975).

11. See Graham Allison, *Essence of Decision* (Boston: Little, Brown and Co., 1971).

12. See Tomas Peñaloza Webb, "El sistema político norteamericano y algunos de sus mecanismos de decisión" (Paper presented at symposium, "Estados Unidos; Un proyecto de investigación," Programa Universitario Justo Sierra, National University of Mexico, April 1983).

Index

About the Book

This book, prepared by the Permanent Secretariat of the Latin American Economic System (SELA), analyzes a range of factors in the current economic policies of the United States that affect Latin American and Caribbean countries. In particular, it pinpoints the effects of U.S. monetary policy on the region's economies and trade relations and on the policies of international financial agencies.